ENCYCLOPEDIA OF AMAZON PARROTS

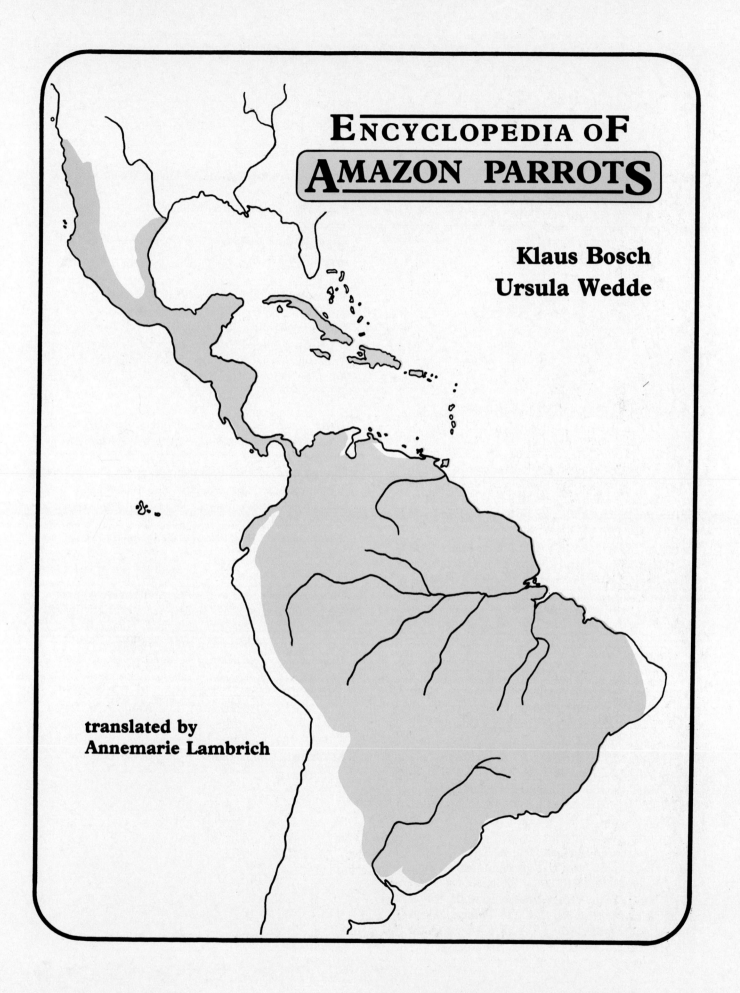

ENCYCLOPEDIA OF
AMAZON PARROTS

Klaus Bosch
Ursula Wedde

translated by
Annemarie Lambrich

Frontispiece: Yellow-crowned Amazon (*A. ochrocephala panamensis*)

Drawings and range maps: Ursula Wedde

Paintings: Jürgen Ritter, Munich (3)

Cages and accessories: Werkfotos Wagner & Keller, Ludwigsburg

Photographs (taken at Vogelpark Walsrode, for the most part): Toni Angermayer (2), Thomas Brosset (7), R. van Dieten (1), Wolfgang de Grahl (8), J. M. Kenning (3), Dr. Claus König (4), Heinz Liebfarth (1), Günther Mühlhaus (2), Horst Müller (51), Ramon Noegel (1), Helen Snyder (1), Noel Snyder (1), Ursula Wedde (7), James Wiley (1).

Thanks to the following for providing photographs of some of the rarer species: Dierenpark Wassenaar, Holland; Jersey Wildlife Preservation Trust, Jersey, Channel Islands; Life Fellowship, Seffner, Florida; Parrot Wildlife Research Project, Rijswijk, Holland; and the U.S. Forest Service Institute of Tropical Forestry, Rio Piedras, Puerto Rico.
Thanks also to Dr. H. E. Wolters for reviewing the systematic table.

Photographs added to the English-language edition: Herbert R. Axelrod, 31, 39, 83—cages courtesy of Bird Depot, Inc. Cliff Bickford, 103, 178. Thomas Brosset, 134 bottom, 158 bottom. Tom Caravaglia, 6, 47, 71, 75, 158 top, 206. Fred Harris, 91 top, 95, 134 top. Ralph Kaehler, 10, 38, 42, 74, 94. Harry V. Lacey, 203. Don Mathews, 179 bottom. Max Mills, 55, 78 top left, 79. A. J. Mobbs, 123. Edward J. Mulawka, 70, 90. Stefan Norberg & Anders Hansson, frontis, 51, 54, 59, 63, 67, 87, 167, 182, 183, 186. Vincent Serbin, 35, 43. Matthew M. Vriends, 130 bottom.

ISBN 0-87666-871-6

Distributed in the UNITED STATES by T.F.H. Publications, Inc., 211 West Sylvania Avenue, Neptune City, NJ 07753; in CANADA by H & L Pet Supplies Inc., 27 Kingston Crescent, Kitchener, Ontario N2B 2T6; Rolf C. Hagen Ltd., 3225 Sartelon Street, Montreal 382 Quebec; in ENGLAND by T.F.H. Publications Limited, 4 Kier Park, Ascot, Berkshire SL5 7DS; in AUSTRALIA AND THE SOUTH PACIFIC by T.F.H. (Australia) Pty. Ltd., Box 149, Brookvale 2100 N.S.W., Australia; in NEW ZEALAND by Ross Haines & Son, Ltd., 18 Monmouth Street, Grey Lynn, Auckland 2 New Zealand; in SINGAPORE AND MALAYSIA by MPH Distributors Pte., 71-77 Stamford Road, Singapore 0617; in the PHILIPPINES by Bio-Research, 5 Lippay Street, San Lorenzo Village, Makati Rizal; in SOUTH AFRICA by Multipet Pty. Ltd., 30 Turners Avenue, Durban 4001. Published by T.F.H. Publications Inc., Ltd. the British Crown Colony of Hong Kong.

Contents

Blue-fronted, Orange-winged, and Mealy Amazons.

Introduction

Why Do Amazons Fascinate Us? There are many motives for bringing amazons into the home. There is, for instance, their talent for mimicry, which probably fascinates most people. But is it only the fact that they can talk and imitate noises and sounds? Or do we like them because they are so affectionate, following our every step, liking nothing more than sitting on our shoulders and letting themselves be petted and scratched? Is it their aptitude for climbing and gymnastics, their great cleverness in overcoming obstacles in the branches, their mastery of the tree with claws and beak? Or is it their droll behavior, into which almost-human traits can be read; their gesturing with beak, wings, and claws; their ability to use the foot as a prehensile organ? Is it their good-natured character, which does not bear grudges, or their friendly manner? Perhaps we are fascinated by their bright eyes, the shimmering plumage, the markings on the head, the "face" which is different in every amazon? Is it because we find their diet as seedeaters unproblematic, their compact excrement practical; or do we enjoy preparing a different menu of seeds, nuts, and fruits daily? Do we observe curiously how, in a group of amazons, a "food taster" tests the new flavors for the others?

Or is it the size of these birds that we consider to be just right, not too small and fragile, so that one has "something in the hand," yet not too large to permit free flight in the home? Is it the green color, the bit of exoticism, the child of the primeval forest which we have brought into our gray world of concrete and which turns us into seafarers and connoisseurs of far-away lands? Or are we stimulated by the challenge of getting a pair of amazons to breed, to participate in their pairing and their family life? Do we desire the look of those two eyes with which the amazon pair watch us curiously, both beaks turned to the same side? Do we like to observe how they yawn at the same time and do almost everything in synchrony? Is it the aura which these parrots radiate, the unmistakable personality of these proud, curious, stubborn, lovable, shrewd, calculating, flattering, lazy, choosy, good- or ill-tempered, grumpy, pert fellows, perplexingly raising their wings?

Amazons are popular for many reasons, and it is indeed possible to take life-long joy in them. Certainly a talent for dealing with animals is required—in any case, a large measure of patience—and *love* for animals. With parrots especially, you do not acquire an automaton that talks when ordered, but a living creature.

The only answer to the question, Which of the animals offered in the trade is absolutely the most reliable talker?, is: Buy yourself a tape recorder! In parrots, mimicry of human speech is only one mode of behavior among many, only a by-product of the close relationship between man and animal. In the wild, parrots do not talk. The fact that amazons learn to talk in captivity has influenced their fate considerably. If they could not do this, they still would be hunted and eaten by Indians, but transport to all corners of the globe would be spared them. On the other hand, their talent for talking helps them to master their fate, because they use it, as we will see, quite successfully to satisfy their requirements. This can be understood as the use of their voices to obtain social contacts. Thus for amazons, talking can have positive results.

For Whom This Book Was Written It often happens that in the beginning there is the wish for a talking hookbill; finally, this becomes a hobby that fills all free time: namely, the keeping and breeding of large parrots and parakeets. This book has been written for all those who are interested in amazons. It should quench that thirst for knowledge one has before making the purchase, as well as that which will certainly develop in the first weeks after one has lived with one's own amazon. The main idea is always that amazons in human care should live as well as possible.

Of course, this book may be the initial inspiration for some readers to acquire an amazon. This desire is not very fortunate for the animals now in the wild. After all, they should be preserved for us in their natural environment. For this reason, this book has also been written for all novice amazon breeders, with whose help it should be possible in the not-too-distant future to meet the demand for amazons. At that time, imports of amazons from their native lands, as of all other wild animals of the earth, can be stopped.

Finally, this book is for all those already familiar with amazons, but who have been looking at the literature in vain for a volume devoted exclusively to amazons. Breeders, dealers, and people with zoological interests will find here all the species and subspecies of amazons.

Some Suggestions About the Use of This Book As far as the names used in this book are concerned, the following must be noted: the names for the species in German are often unclear. These names, just like the English, French, etc., are "trivial names" arising in the course of time. The scientific (Latin) name alone is definitive. In German, for instance, it can happen that one species, *Amazona albifrons*, is called by two names: "White-fronted Amazon" and "Spectacled Amazon." Or one name is used for several species: "Blue-fronted Amazon" for *Amazona aestiva* and *Amazona versicolor*. Only the scientific name is unmistakable.

When *sub*species are distinguished (another word for these is *races*), another name is added —for example: *Amazona albifrons saltuensis*. For the subspecies first named, the nominate form, the name of the species is repeated: *Amazona albifrons albifrons*.

English names are also listed, because they give added information to fanciers about distinctive characteristics. Thus, the two species of amazons living in Jamaica, *Jamaika-Amazone* (*Amazona collaria*) and *Rotspiegelamazone* ("Red-speculum," *Amazona agilis*) are called Yellow-billed and Black-billed amazons in British and American usage, after the yellow and black coloration of their beaks. [Similarly, in this

English-language edition, German names have been included when they provide information of interest. Literal translations of German names are enclosed in quotation marks.—Ed.]

Historical Facts from the Literature A hundred years ago, in 1881, the Creutz'sche Verlagsbuchhandlung in Magdeburg published the book *Die Papageien* by Dr. Karl Russ. In 1896, Russ brought out *Die Amazonenpapageien*, and in 1898, *Die Sprechenden Papageien*. In these volumes, Russ dealt systematically with the amazons, which were named amazon parrots by him at that time. Dr. Finsch had called them short-winged parrots; Brehm called them green parrots. In the jargon of traders and sailors, they were called *Kriken*, derived from the French word *criquer*, "to screech."

At that time, amazons were already vended as talking birds, but a much larger number were hunted by the Indians for their tasty meat and their colorful plumage. They were eaten like chickens and pigeons, in broth with rice. It was also known that young amazons which had been taken from the nest showed a great talent for mimicry. These animals were sold to sailors in the port cities. The Double Yellow-headed Amazon (*Amazona ochrocephala oratrix*) was considered the best talker, followed by the Blue-fronted Amazon (*Amazona aestiva*), the Yellow-crowned Amazon (*Amazona ochrocephala ochrocephala*) and the Yellow-naped Amazon (*Amazona ochrocephala auropalliata*). Among all species of amazons there were completely untalented animals, which were called *Uhlis*. An *Uhli* was an amazon that the seller or dealer was convinced would not learn to talk even with the best care and treatment. Such animals cost about 8–10 marks. Prices amounted to 15–30 marks for average birds; for rare species, 60–75 marks; for hand-tame, talking birds, 90–150 marks. In special instances, the price was as much as 300 marks. The Yellow-shouldered Amazon (*Amazona barbadensis*), also called "Little Yellowhead" or "Sun Parrot," was often imported. This amazon was considered a lovable, easily and cheaply aquired pet. Today it is on the list of endangered species.

At that time the feeding of captive amazons was considerably different from today. As the main staple, they were given hemp. Sunflower seeds in large amounts were considered dangerous and were fed at most as a special treat. Sailors and traders, lacking seeds, gave them rolls soaked in coffee and tea. But Russ considered this method of feeding harmful, and blamed it, among other things, for the deaths among the animals during transport. The sea crossing lasted for weeks on a steamer, months on a sailing ship. In the European port cities, the amazons were taken over by so-called trainers, who taught them to speak. These were mostly innkeepers in sailors' bars, former sailors, or barbers. In *Die sprechenden Papageien*, Russ expressed regret that the amazons picked up from these people "swearwords, vulgar expressions, or other repulsive sounds, such as feigning the cough of a consumptive, snoring, rattling, spitting, and such"—habits which later could not be broken.

Russ noted that amazons with blue and yellow markings on their heads could be mistaken for one another, and alluded to the possibility of differentiation by means of the bend of the wing. He regretted that Linnaeus in his time had given the name Amazon Parrot to the bird with the green bend of the wing (*Amazona amazonica*); since then, however, the species with red on the bend of the wing had been observed much more frequently, so the name should belong to it, if not to the entire genus. He tried to clarify matters by introducing the name "Venezuelan Amazon" for *Amazona amazonica*, since at that time these birds reached us mainly from Venezuela. The other species he called "amazon parrot with the red bend of the wing, or the Common Amazon" (*Amazona aestiva*). Thus arose our present names *Venezuela-Amazone* (*Amazona amazonica*) and *Rotbugamazone* ("Red-bend," *Amazona aestiva*); but the latter is also called *Blaustirnamazone* ("Blue-fronted Amazon").

Above: Blue-fronted Amazon *(A. aestiva).*

Facing page: Advertisements from the periodical *Die Gefiederte Welt,* the year 1889:

Parrot!! Blue-fronted Amazon, 1½ years old, wonderfully tame, comes immediately to the finger, goes in and out of its cage (never bites!), gives kisses and [offers] its foot, already says several words, very intelligent and teachable, a quite amusing and sociable animal for ladies and children, quite perky and healthy, is for sale for 35 marks, together with its still quite new and elegant cage for 45 marks. Shipped cash on delivery, good arrival guaranteed. Replies to F.R. 10, care of *Die Gefiederte Welt.* (211)

———————

Grey Parrot (Jako) with quite new, excellent salon cage for sale for 30 marks. It has been here for ½ year, is used to all food and water, whistles very nicely, and is beginning to talk. Shipped cash on delivery with guarantee of safe arrival. (214)
F. Rejsek, Hamburg, Alter Steinweg 56.

11

Life in the Wild

Distribution To understand the behavior of amazons in captivity, one must always look to others of the species living in the wild in Central and South America. According to Forshaw, amazons inhabit the most diverse landscapes there: dense rain forests, open woodlands, steppes and savannahs, riverine lowlands and swampy coasts, estuaries of rivers, as well as high plateaus and mountain slopes. They have been observed in flocks, i.e., groups from five to thirty, or even hundreds of animals.

Mixed flocks have also been sighted: in Jamaica, Yellow-billed Amazons (*Amazona collaria*) and Black-billed Amazons (*Amazona agilis*) were seen flying together. In Mexico, White-fronted Amazons (*Amazona albifrons*) were seen together with Yellow-lored Amazons (*Amazona xantholora*). As a rule, however, separate groups are homogenous.

The species *Amazona ochrocephala*, i.e., the Yellow-crowned Amazon with all its subspecies, has a very large geographical distribution from Mexico to Brazil, while the Festive Amazon (*Amazona festiva*) occurs only in a narrowly limited area. The Scaly-naped Amazon (*Amazona mercenaria*) is the mountain bird among the amazons. The Blue-cheeked Amazon (*Amazona dufresniana rhodocorytha*), fleeing cultivation, has retired to the Brazilian highlands. A typical inhabitant of the savannah is the Yellow-faced Amazon (*Amazona xanthops*).

Food Acquisition If amazons appear in cultivated areas, the damage they cause to fruit plantations and grain fields is considerable. They are killed by the farmers, caught with nets, or, at the very least, chased away. Amazons are good flyers. Once they take off, screeching and crowing loudly, they fly very high and over long distances. In flight, they sound their typical, shrill calls. When they discover a new source of food, such as a tree with young buds, they alight with loud cackling. The branches bend under the weight of the birds. Then the hooked beaks start their work. Only a small part of what is bitten off is swallowed. Young shoots and pieces of bark are ground in the beak, and traces of plant juices are consumed in the process. When the trees bear fruits or nuts, the tastiest ones are preferred. The amazon's foot serves as a hand and holds the fruit. It has been noted that the left foot is more often used for prehension than the right. The beak searches first for a kernel or pit in the interior of the fruit. This is freed from the flesh and cracked. Then comes the fruit; both flesh and juice are taken. When a branch is thus completely stripped, the amazon tries, if at all possible, to reach its next bit of food by climbing. Once in a tree, it does not fly. While they are eating, the group of amazons remain silent. Only individual animals which are already satisfied utter a soft murmuring. At the end of the meal, all sharpen their lower mandibles: a strange sound (*schraft-schraft*) is created by rubbing the lower mandible against the horny ridges of the upper. In this manner the edge of the lower mandible becomes sharp again, because it has been dulled by working on hard foods. It was believed previously that the amazons were ruminating. Indeed, occasionally seeds which have not been chewed are brought up; however, this is the action not of the beak, but of the gizzard.

Forshaw writes that throughout all this the amazons are very watchful. Amazons that live near human settlements are even more cautious than their relatives that live in untouched forest areas. If a human approaches a group of amazons, he does not even suspect their presence at first. In the foliage their green color is a perfect camouflage. The amazons, however, noticed the "enemy" long before and eye him curiously. Suddenly they take off with great screeching, startling the unsuspecting visitor. In one instance reported, the amazons waited until the enemy passed without noticing them, before taking off into the air.

With the Puerto Rican Amazon (*Amazona vittata*), Dr. Kepler, director of the Luquillo National Forest in Puerto Rico, observed several signal cries: command to fly, call during flight, and contact calls. The latter are uttered by pairs either in turn or simultaneously in duet. In this manner, amazons communicate over great distances if members of the group become separated.

Amazons always fly the same route to feeding places, until the supply of food is exhausted. Then they move on, but not without inspecting the old feeding places from time to time and harvesting the newly grown vegetation. If their flight path leads over a mountain on which drenching rain is falling or which is covered by fog, they will make detours through the valleys to arrive at their destination dry (Forshaw).

Reproduction Amazons are cavity breeders. They find suitable cavities, preferably from six to fifteen meters above the ground, in large trees where branches have broken off and in woodpecker holes, in rotted palm trunks, and in holes in rocks. Openings facing south are preferred because of the shelter from the wind. The interior is first cleared out; nesting material is not carried in. The opening is between 10 cm. and 23 cm. in diameter, the depth between 43 cm. and 64 cm.

Once a pair have found one another, this marriage is valid for life. If one dies, the other will remarry. Both search for a suitable nesting site, work it somewhat with their beaks if necessary, and proceed, usually between February and June, to breed. Once chosen, the nesting hole is used by a pair year after year. The clutch contains two to four pure white eggs, which the female incubates for about four weeks (Low: 28 days; Forshaw: 25–30 days). The hatched young remain in the nest cavity sixty to seventy-five days before they leave it for the first time. The male stays outside and feeds the female. According to the Nottebohms (Forshaw), an Orange-winged Amazon male (*Amazona amazonica*) was observed in the evenings leaving the nest site and flying to the communal roost; it is doubtful that this behavior is usual.

Breeding is only fifty percent successful because enemies destroy the eggs and because many eggs are infertile. With two to four eggs per clutch, only one or two young hatch. These continue to be threatened by nest robbers, by decayed giant trees falling, or by rainwater seeping into the nest cavity causing death by drowning. While predatory felids, rats, and other vermin endanger eggs and hatchlings, birds of prey like the Red-tailed Hawk (*Buteo jamaicensis*), for instance, are among the enemies of the adult amazons. On volcanic islands they are menaced by eruptions. Tornados destroy feeding and breeding places, and the displaced amazons are victimized by hunting natives.

Roosting Sites In the evening, the flocks seek out particular trees for sleeping. All amazons from a given area use the same tree or group of trees. In the tropics, particularly near the equator, there are twelve hours of daylight and twelve hours of night all year long. The amazons are accustomed to this rhythm. As the parties arrive, the wrangling for the best

The flight pattern of amazons resembles that of ducks.

perches begins anew with every incoming group, accompanied by loud screeching. But finally quiet descends on the flock of amazons, and the screeching gives way to an unvoiced gurgling. The animals continue this even after they have turned their heads back, hidden their beaks in their feathers, and pulled up one leg. If the sleeping group is startled by something, a fluttering sound spreads through the branches. Each amazon abruptly fluffs up its feathers, shaking off dewdrops and dust; the flight apparatus is readied, just in case. The fluffing of one single bird is sufficient stimulus to cause the same reaction in all the others. At dawn, noise begins again in the amazons' tree. The rising sun is greeted with screeching; all screech as loudly as they can. It is time to leave. Little by little, small groups take off from the treetops and scatter in all directions to look for food.

Species Threatened by Extinction The island species are more threatened with extinction than others. They must flee civilization again and again, retreating to areas inaccessible to humans: the marshes on the coast or the craggy interior of the island. They have to share this reduced environment with other species; the result is a decline in population. When it's almost too late, the nations they inhabit establish nature preserves and prohibit exports. The Washington Convention [Convention on International Trade in Endangered Species of Wild Fauna and Flora (CITES)] forbids trade in endangered species. These parrots should be preserved for the world while a few individuals still remain in their native environment. The Federal Republic of Germany also signed the Washington Convention in 1976. According to the most recent listing (1981) the following amazons are protected:

1. St. Vincent Amazon, *Amazona guildingii*
2. Imperial Amazon, *Amazona imperialis*
3. Yellow-shouldered Amazon, *Amazona barbadensis*
4. Red-necked Amazon, *A. arausiaca*
5. Cuban Amazon, *Amazona leucocephala*
6. Vinaceous Amazon, *Amazona vinacea*
7. Blue-cheeked Amazon, *Amazona dufresniana rhodocorytha*
8. Red-spectacled Amazon, *Amazona pretrei*
9. Puerto Rican Amazon, *Amazona vittata*
10. St. Lucia Amazon, *Amazona versicolor*

Cuban Amazon (A. leucocephala)

Der weißköpfige Amazonenpapagei mit rothem Bauchfleck
[Psittacus leucocéphalus].

Der Flug geht geradeaus schnell vorwärts, aber mit vielen Flügelschlägen. Wenn man einen oder einige heruntergeschossen hat oder wenn gar einer verwundet ist und schreit, so kommen (wie bei den europäischen Krähen u. a.) viele herbei, und der Jäger hat die beste Gelegenheit, noch eine reiche Beute zu machen. Sie setzen oder hängen sich gern an die jungen, noch stangenförmig emporstehenden Palmblätter, auch an freie, dürre oder doch blattlose Aeste und klettern an denselben. Im April suchen sie Baumlöcher und todte Palmen, welche hohl sind oder seitliche Löcher haben, z. B. frühere Nester von Spechten auf, um in dieselben ihre drei bis vier Eier zu legen. Die Nistzeit währt bis zum Juli." Obwol er fast nur in der erwähnten Weise gezähmt in den Handel gelangt, so sind bisher doch erst wenige Erfahrungen inbetreff seiner veröffentlicht worden. Herr A. Creutz in Stettin gibt eine kurze, doch wol etwas überschwängliche Schilderung: „Er gehört zu den klügsten Vögeln der Erde, denn er zeichnet sich durch Verstand, leichte Fassungsgabe und vorzügliches Gedächtniß zugleich aus; darum lernt er

Excerpts from the original text of Russ, p. 559
(quoting Dr. Gundlach):

**The White-headed Amazon Parrot
with a Red Abdominal Spot
(*Psittacus leucocéphalus*)**

"Forward flight is rapid, in a straight line, but with many wing beats. If one or several have been shot down, or particularly if one has been injured and cries out, many will come near (as do European crows, among others), and the hunter has the best opportunity to make a rich bag. They like to sit or hang on the young palm leaves still sticking up like poles, or on free, dry, or at least leafless branches, and climb on them. In April they seek tree cavities and dead palms which are hollow or have holes in their sides (i.e., old woodpecker nests), to lay their three to four eggs in them. The breeding season lasts into July." Even though it almost always reaches the trade tamed in the manner described, only few experiences concerning it have been published thus far. Herr A. Creutz of Stettin gives a brief but probably somewhat exaggerated description: "It belongs among the most intelligent birds on earth because it excels in understanding, ease of learning, and outstand ing memory; thus it learns . . ."

The Way to Us

Capture of Young Animals As previously mentioned, once hatched, amazon babies remain in the tree cavity for sixty to seventy-five days. It is during this time that they are taken out by Indians. A soft, nourishing gruel, prepared from cooked potatoes or corn, is stuffed into the beaks of the young animals. This chore is done mainly by women, since the men have taken the animals from their nests. Perhaps this is why amazons trust women more than men. It is always men who grasp them again and again, during capture or to transfer them from one transport container to another. During these days of hand-rearing, some young animals still have a soft beak which can easily be deformed during feeding. Thus, one occasionally finds a pushed-in beak among the amazon babies when they reach us, a cosmetic flaw which is usually not a handicap for the animal.

At this age amazons are not beautiful anyway. Their first plumage is naturally rather thin, both in terms of bulk and color. The green camouflage color is predominant, as protection for the still inexperienced offspring, but the blue, yellow, white, and red markings, which become important only with sexual maturity, are not very evident. The juvenile Yellow-naped Amazon (*Amazona ochrocephala auropalliata*), for instance, has no yellow nape as yet; the Yellow-crowned Amazon *Amazona ochrocephala belizensis* has yellow only on the forehead and crown. The fact that the feathers are not as sturdy as those of the adult birds may be caused by the one-sided diet, but it is probably also a matter of constitution. In any case, the plumage of young birds always looks a little disheveled, worn, and incomplete when they reach the pet shops here. How well an amazon's plumage comes through transport and quarantine depends too on its strength and stamina.

Behavior of Young Animals It is already decided in the nest cavity which amazons will

survive. The young hatch at intervals of a few days, and the firstborn will always have an advantage in development. It will grow to be more courageous, aggressive, poised, and stronger physically. Later, when being fed by human hands, it will still be dominant, pushing away the weaker ones. Confident, robust amazons are best able to keep their feathers well groomed in spite of the hardships of the long journey. The tail feathers of amazons are often damaged; sometimes they are completely missing. But they have not been cut back by humans. The cause is to be found in the fact that many amazons are forced to always stand on the floor of the container because their presence on the perches is not tolerated by the ones sitting there. However, Nature has fully prepared the amazons to take care of their tails. When turning around in tight places, they cleverly turn the tail upward without bumping it into anything; when they "stride" in the grass or similar places, they cross their wings on the back in order to be able to hold the tail as high as possible. Only in unusual situations will they cease to protect or groom their plumage because their attention is drawn to other things.

Also among the young amazons are some very alert, constantly active ones that have a strong need for contact. These intelligent, speech-talented animals investigate every square inch of their cage, climb up and down on the wires, and are incessantly active. This, together with the vertical wiring, above all causes the tail feathers to be damaged. Bedraggled amazons, therefore, are by no means undesirable animals. They include on one hand more compliant, less forceful birds which will become tame more quickly; on the other hand are intelligent animals which have a pronounced need for contact.

Capture of Adults in the Wild Amazons that have already lived long years of their lives in their natural environment are caught as well. They are captured with nets or, as P. Deimer writes, drugged with sulphur fumes, which are fanned under the trees until the birds fall down insensible. This sounds callous, and is, like all animal capture, a matter which quickly inflames tempers. Buy one must consider that those using this method are interested only in catching birds in the safest way possible. Horst Stern said once on a TV show that the person who points an outraged finger at the animal trapper should remember that four fingers of his hand are pointing back at him as the purchaser. Another thing should not be forgotten: those amazons which are hunted and killed in their native lands for damaging crops would be better off captured and put into aviaries.

With animals caught in the wild, it must be taken into consideration that they were already firmly paired, perhaps had already raised young, and had a command of intraspecific communication. Perhaps they were even leaders of a flock, or signalled when enemies approached the roosting tree. Such amazons are more difficult to handle during transport and quarantine. A wing is clipped so that they cannot get away. Sometimes they are left unclipped, but then they run the danger of getting their wings caught. After all, an amazon which opens its wings fully has a wingspread of 60 cm. Sometimes both wings are clipped, but not as frequently.

Behavior of Adults Captured in the Wild
Captured adult animals react variously to their new situation. Some come to terms with it quickly; others need a longer time in order to change. They use their loud voices, in any case. They call for their mates or utter alarm calls. In fright or panic, especially when faced with a direct threat, they may show a tendency toward "corner sitting," i.e., they go to the floor of the cage and squeeze their tails into a corner. Sometimes they will lock both legs into the corner of the cage and press their backs against the wire. Abdomen and beak are presented to the presumed attacker. Really frightened animals will lie on their backs. These forget completely to use their beaks as defense; full of fear, they don't even bite. In these moments they are completely indifferent to the condition of their plumage. However, such birds are exceptions. Amazons learn a lot from each other. If a courageous one considers a situation no longer threatening and approaches the food dish fearlessly and eats, this has a calming effect on the frightened one and provides a good example. The bird adopts this behavior and overcomes its initial shyness.

Importation and Quarantine [In Germany] The amazons are now brought to central collection points where the state of their health is evaluated. An importation permit is given only if the official veterinarian of the exporting country certifies the good health of the birds. In addition, the amazons must not belong to a protected species and there must not be any danger of an acute epizootic in the exporting country. Then follows the transport by air, which is considerably faster than a hundred years ago, when the amazons reached us by boat. However, the change of climate hits them more suddenly. In our airports, the amazons are immediately isolated in the quarantine rooms. From there, they come to the special quarantine stations of the individual importers. They are kept in quarantine for at least eight weeks.

The prophylactic treatment against psittacosis required by law lasts for forty-five days. During this time, the amazons are given a broad-spectrum antibiotic with their food. By this method, psittacosis is prevented with a probability bordering on certainty. Whether the treatment was successful is proved by tests of droppings or blood. The healthy animals receive an official leg band with a serial number. The importer can now pass them on to the dealers. The high dosage of antibiotics does not, however, preclude all illnesses, as a recent investigation by Dr. M. Heidenreich has shown. Thirty-one amazons, 28 Grey Parrots and 11 Sulphur-crested Cockatoos—70 parrots altogether —were observed for half a year following the 45-day treatment with antibiotics. During that

Noel Snyder installing a nesting cavity for the
Puerto Rican Amazon (*A. vittata*).

Tucuman Amazons (*A. tucumana*) in flight, in the province of Salta in northwest Argentina.

time, 18 animals died of the following diseases: 12 of aspergillosis, 2 of *Pasteurella* infections, 1 of a mixed bacterial infection, 1 of gout, 1 of trichomoniasis, and 1 of a heavy infestation with tapeworms. The cause lies with the reduced resistance of the badly stressed quarantine birds. In a parallel-testing experiment, a special food in slightly damp, granular form was offered in addition to the usual seed mixture. This helped to reduce the incidence of the losses by half (*Die Voliere*, 81/2).

These numbers should not prevent the potential purchaser from buying an amazon from a pet shop. If it gets there, it is an amazon which has weathered the stress well; otherwise it would not be there. The longer an amazon is to be seen in a shop, the less likely it has a disease. Moreover, for the sake of trade alone, ill birds are immediately treated by a veterinarian. During this long period "behind the scenes," the adult amazons, initially half-wild, become somewhat tame, while the youngsters, initially completely tame, temporarily lose a little of their tameness.

Banding As already mentioned, all amazons must be banded with a leg band. Banding, like the registration and maintenance during quarantine, is exactly prescribed by law. For the private amazon keeper, these ordinances also have a certain importance. At the time of purchase, the buyer must give his name and address, and this information is entered into a register by the seller. If the amazon was not bought for the purpose of breeding or resale, and if no trips abroad are planned with it, no other ordinances must be observed by the owner, except that an outbreak of psittacosis must be reported. It is permissible to remove the annoying band from the leg of one's pet; however, it should not be thrown away, but simply stored in a safe place. The band is tangible proof that the bird underwent an official quarantine.

Breeding Permit If the amazon keeper wants to breed these parrots, he will have to register this intent with the proper officials, usually the city or county authorities. The amazons have to wear leg bands, and a register must be kept. This applies even to the smallest hobby breeding of parrots and parakeets of any species. In such situations, an appointed veterinarian will check the breeding facilities and the knowledgeability of the applicant. The officials will require a certificate of good conduct, bands and registers must be purchased, and a quarantine room must be set up. Altogether, certification as a breeder can be as expensive as half a driver's license.

Vacations Abroad One statute is important for all amazon owners who want to take their pets along on trips abroad. Among other things, it contains the provision that a private person may take up to three parrots from the German Federal Republic abroad and back again, without subjecting the animals to a quarantine upon their return and without needing an import permit. The owner, however, must not be a dealer or a breeder. In principle, official certification of the identity of the keeper and a statement of the species, colors, markings, and band numbers of the animals is sufficient. When returning, the identity of the animals will have to be proved to customs officials. Arrival and departure have to take place within twelve months. However, since an official veterinary certificate of health is usually required for entry into other countries (information can be obtained at the consulates), these certificates can also suffice for the German officials, providing the information described above is stated in the German language.

Things to Know When Buying

Matters of Conscience Beforehand The acquisition of an amazon must be considered carefully. One should not entertain the thought that the animal can always be resold if it does not fulfill one's expectations. Even the idea that, lacking a buyer, the amazon can always be given to a zoo is mistaken. R. Low writes that English zoos are offered hundreds of parrots annually by owners who feel overburdened. It is very doubtful that zoos will accept these animals. Fortunately, prices of DM700 and up tend to check impulse buying. One should never purchase an amazon as a gift for someone else; the future owner has to shoulder this concern. Once the plan to buy is firm, one should no longer hesitate. The first step is to visit many animal dealers. One should also visit the nearest zoo and observe the amazons there. One should not buy the first animal he sees, rather the one that stands out in comparison with others.

One should not give in to the temptation to take the easy way out and have an amazon shipped to one's house—and not because parrot mail-order houses are basically untrustworthy! These shippers do their absolute best. But in matters concerning a parrot, all laziness and thoughtlessness must be avoided as much as possible. If, at the time of purchase, which is a period of increased interest in the animal, one cannot be bothered to pick it up or select it in person, how can one expect to care for it a year later? The same is true if someone purchases an amazon in a local pet shop and insists to the salesperson that the store should keep the animal for the next two weeks (over the holidays, for instance). It is not rare to see a tag saying Sold on the cage of an amazon. One wonders whether the buyer was serious about his purchase. Won't the amazon be in the way on the next ski weekend or the next swimming holiday?

If, for whatever reason, purchase is made from a mail-order house, it should be done during a time of moderate weather, i.e., spring or fall. The amazon will be placed into a shipping container on a thick layer of bird seed, and pieces of apple will be added to counter thirst. The railroad employees sometimes volunteer to look after the screeching travelers by giving them an occasional drink of water. "Last watered at — o'clock," they write on the shipping container. After all, it can happen that the amazon will travel for a full two days, especially over the long distances which are too far for travel by car.

Idiosyncracies of Amazons Amazons require contact with a group or with a partner. The keeper should, if possible, be home all day long. It is not sufficient if other members of the family feed and water the bird during the day, but have no other interest in it. If you are the kind of person who would rather sit in his own backyard than go out, an amazon is the right companion for you! They are not recommended for children, whose interest in it will soon diminish. Later, as teenagers and young adults, they will naturally have other interests than a cage or aviary bird. A Budgerigar is more suitable for children, since it will not live that long. Amazons are not so extremely conservative as the Grey Parrot, but they too need some time to adapt to changes. This requires patience on the part of the keeper.

An amazon will talk only when it is completely relaxed, certainly not always on command, and, above all, not always what one wants to hear One should not expect, therefore, to have it repeat every word like a tape recorder. Many amazons learn quite a lot, but there is no guarantee of this. Even without talking, they can be very entertaining.

Amazons very much need exercise. They want to climb, fly, and run. One should have suitably rustic furnishings, not a museum. Parrots gnaw a lot and constantly require new climbing trees,

Rain forest in the upper Amazon basin: in the vicinity of the Rio Napo in eastern Ecuador.

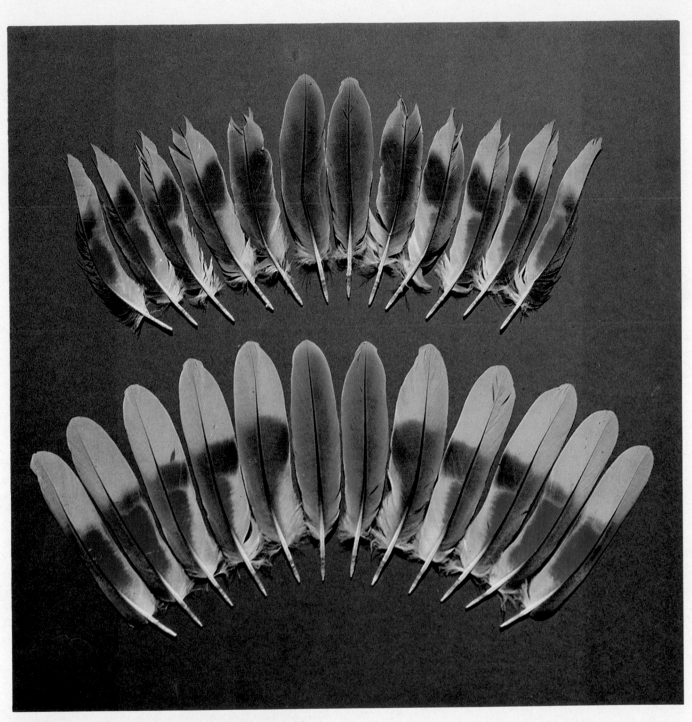

Tail feathers of the Yellow-crowned Amazon (*A. ochrocephala ochrocephala*). Upper row: feathers from the time of purchase, at about one year of age. Lower row: Feathers worn two years later. The red is weak in the earlier feathers, becoming more extensive later; meanwhile, the central band of green has decreased.

twigs, and branches, which first must be obtained. This is not simple in a city, and even in the country one cannot take home parts of trees and bushes without prior permission.

Parrots will never be completely housebroken. One will have to expect droppings on the carpet or put paper over particularly liable spots. Amazons will strew remnants of their meals all over the floor, pick off feather dust and down, and in the course of flight movements will raise dust from the cage floor. With aviary birds these matters of cleanliness are not significant. However, there are other problems outdoors. Amazons can become quite noisy, particularly during courtship. During the morning and evening hours especially, they raise their voices. Therefore, one needs a remote house or friendly neighbors.

Having considered all of this, if you still persist in your desire to keep amazons, then you must be counted among the thousands of parrot lovers throughout the world, people who are crazy about amazons.

Selecting a Bird When you stand in front of a cage containing several amazons, the choice can be very difficult. The salesperson will place several animals in turn on your hands, arms, and shoulders, and the bright fellows will climb all over you, gnaw on your wristwatch, try to get to buttons, and sensitively test a finger held in front of a beak. If one tries to pet them, they squeak grumpily or readily present a ruffled nape. A particularly courageous amazon tries to pinch your nose, while another takes off unexpectedly and lands on the floor. This scenario presumes you are dealing with young amazons; you can try to ascertain this by asking the following questions:

- Is the plumage dull, with washed-out colors, still not fully colored?
- Are the scales on the legs and claws small, soft, and flat?
- Is the iris very dark or pale?
- Is the beak smooth, without several horny layers?

If the answer to all of these questions is yes, then you are dealing with a young amazon. The salesperson will confirm this. If the amazon is to be tame, it is advantageous to purchase a young animal. However, older animals also can become tame. Only so far as talking is concerned are older animals obviously less desirable than young ones. For this reason, the young ones are more expensive.

Now check its state of health:

- Does the animal have all of its claws and toes?
- Is the beak well formed and not broken off?
- Are the nostrils open, not clogged?
- Are both eyes open, the lids not sticking?
- Can it see with both eyes?
- Can it fold its wings properly; does either wing hang?
- Is the animal picked bald anywhere?
- Is the breast well fleshed?
- Is the vent clean and dry, not messy?
- Are the droppings in the cage well formed?

Bare spots are usually explained away by saying that the animal is molting. Parrots molt continually; new feathers are always growing in, and others fall out, without causing baldness. Whether the breast is strong can be tested by touching or by blowing back the feathers. The keel of the sternum must not stick out like a knife; this is a sign of malnutrition. After eating fruit, the droppings can sometimes be damp to liquid. Droppings excreted while a bird is excited are sometimes that way too.

A good animal dealer will certainly not sell a sick animal knowingly. From time to time, however, an amazon with a missing claw may be offered at a reduced price. If the animal is suitable in other ways, one should take it, because the missing claw will not handicap it significantly. For a breeding cock, however, it might make for difficulties during copulation.

According to Pinter, the nutritional state can be assessed by weighing. First one weighs the empty cage, then it should be weighed with the animal inside. Pinter lists the following normal weights for amazons:

- Small amazons, such as
  Amazona albifrons   200–250 g.
- *Amazona amazonica* and
  similar species   320–370 g.
- *Amazona ochrocephala
  ochrocephala* and the like   340–420 g.
- *Amazona aestiva,* depending
  on size   400–550 g.
- Large amazons, like *Amazona
  farinosa*   650–850 g.

Much depends on the size and the age of the animal. The species mentioned give only a general guideline.

Condition of the Plumage As mentioned previously, many amazons, particularly wild ones, have had their wings clipped in their country of origin. The most radical method is the one where one cuts across the back of the bird when its wings are closed, thereby cutting all feathers, even the green coverts, in half. The animals then sit there with their rumps uncovered. Such amazons look awlful and do not feel pleased with an exposed back. Fortunately, this method is rarely practiced. More frequently, amazons arriving here have only one wing clipped. When they attempt to fly, they lose their balance and flap to the ground. This can cause injuries. The remaining flight feathers on the other wing do not help, because each beat of the wings produces unequal forces right and left, which puts the bird off balance. Sometimes it cannot even flutter to the ground with any degree of control. This, however, should still be possible for a clipped animal. Therefore, to avoid unpleasant surprises later, one should inquire of the dealer whether and how the bird has been clipped.

If one wants to have a flighted bird clipped, this can be done right at the pet shop. It should be made clear that both wings should be trimmed. If one would like to handle the scissors oneself, however, all the necessary information can be found in a later chapter.

The opposite will more often be the case; namely, that the purchaser acquires a clipped bird and hopes the feathers will grow in.

However, this is not always as unproblematic as the layman imagines. If the wing feathers have been trimmed excessively, individual feathers will grow back at fairly long intervals but are soon lost again. The reason: they break during premature attempts at flying or during emergency landings. These single feathers also catch easily when the amazon climbs. Any unusually strained feather will fall off one day, since it lacks the neighboring feathers which would support and hold it while it grows in. In such cases, it can take years before the flight feathers are all grown in again. Because cut feathers are not used much, they will not fall out for a long time. The dropping of a feather is the prerequisite for a new one growing in. So, many bird keepers reach for the pliers in these cases. This procedure is very painful for the bird. The distress can be spread out a little if one pulls only one clipped feather per week. It is not necessary to pull the feathers on both left and right wings. Russ writes that the corresponding feather on the opposite side will fall out after a short time and thus does not have to be pulled out.

The authors reject pulling the feathers as a matter of principle. The laws for the protection of animals prohibit causing pain, suffering, or damage to an animal without reasonable grounds. While it may seem that acceleration of feather growth is an adequate reason, it poses problems, particularly during the period of acclimatization, to force a bird into molting, which is the production of horny substances by the body. This is even less advisable for a parrot which has yet to be tamed than for an aviary bird.

In rare instances it may be that the site of feather growth has been damaged. This occurs when the bird flutters a lot, constantly banging its clipped primaries against the wires of the cage. The first few primaries will not grow in again, and the animal will remain incapable of flight for the rest of its life. Worn tail feathers are the quickest to grow back. One should make certain, however, that they were not bitten off by the animal, but were really broken or worn off from other causes. It will be better

from the outset if a novice does not buy a
feather biter or plucker.

Lastly, the dealer should be asked how long
he has had the amazon in his shop and whether
it has had close association with other amazons
in the cage, even if they have already been sold.

When an agreement has been reached, one
should also buy a bag of the bird food regularly
fed, to keep the amazon from having to make
too many adjustments all at once.

Transporting the bird home can be done in
the cage, if it is bought at the same time, or in
a sturdy carton with a lid. A new era in the life
of the amazon—and in yours—is beginning.

**The Rio Napo in the Amazon basin in eastern
Ecuador, home of several amazon species.**

26

Primary and secondary flight feathers of a Yellow-crowned Amazon (*A. ochrocephala ochrocephala*). The red speculum is easy to see.

Tertial feathers of a Yellow-crowned Amazon (*A. ochrocephala ochrocephala*).

27

Accommodations

Some Basics About the Care of Amazons

Amazons are social animals; they have an innate need for contact. If two or more amazons are kept together, they are interested less in their keeper than in companions of their own species. In this case, they rarely learn human speech. Someone who doesn't value this accomplishment can still observe many other interesting modes of behavior and can enjoy them. Groups of amazons require a large aviary with a shelter room, or a room of their own in the house. In brief, much room but only a little time is required.

The fact that amazons become somewhat loud mornings and evenings must be considered from the very beginning. Only when eggs or young are in the nest box do they refrain from screeching. Of course, there are loud and not-so-loud amazons of all species. Within a group of amazons, one lively, noisy animal is enough to stimulate the others to squawk, too. Moreover, during breeding season, amazons exhibit a tendency to attack, so that it may be an advantage if the food dishes can be reached from the outside.

To the amazon kept as a tame single bird, the most beautiful bird room and the largest aviary is relatively unimportant. It will constantly yearn for its keeper or other members of the family. In contrast to the group situation, one needs much time and little room (the meaning of "little" follows in the next chapter). Someone should keep the amazon company for at least half the day. To play with it for an hour or two in the evening is not enough. During this time, the amazon must be permitted out of its cage. It needs perches in the house to which it can fly or where it can be put. It will also want to be taken along outdoors. Amazons that cannot fly are quite manageable in this situation; they allow themselves to be carried on the shoulder. They should not be put on the branches of tall trees, however, because they will continue to

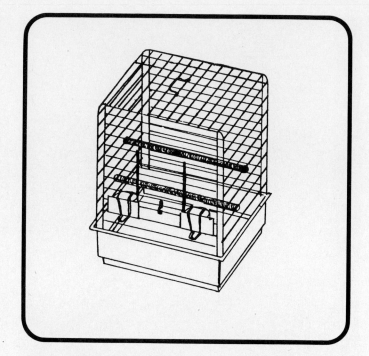

Above: With horizontal wiring, perches can be placed at various heights, and the bird can climb up and down the sides of the cage. Unlike the cage shown on the facing page, here the perches are placed correctly: parallel to one another.

Below: This cage of washable hardboard protects the amazon from drafts and the floor from dirt, but also isolates the animal from its surroundings unnecessarily. It measures 74 x 46 x 75 cm., with chrome-plated wiring, a tray, and places for three dishes.

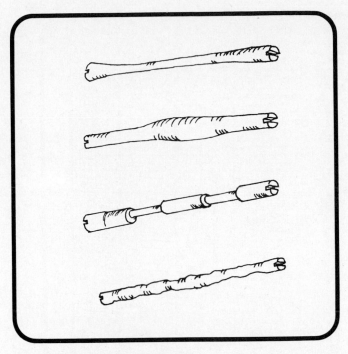

Above: Various perch shapes.

Below: Parrot cage, 45 x 45 x 75 cm., brass- or chrome-plated wiring, horizontal on front and back only.

climb upward and will not come down of their own free will. Tame amazons which can fly should be taken outside in the cage. It is better if they are put on a parrot chain, which may be obtained in pet shops, during this time (see also the section on wing clipping).

The Cage: *1. SHAPE AND DIMENSIONS*
The cage should be rectangular, to keep the bird from getting the so-called turning disease, a nervous turning and twisting of the head caused by the lack of orientation within the wire circle. There are some very nice-looking cages whose four walls are bent and come together at the top. The dimensions should not be less than 40 x 40 x 60 cm. If the amazon is taken out frequently, it will not require a much larger cage. Since a tame and talking amazon should be taken along when visiting friends or going on trips by car, the cage should fit into the car. Having both a large room cage and a small travel cage is optimal. The cage wires should run horizontally so the amazon can climb around more easily.

2. PERCHES The perches that come with the cage are too smooth and do not offer a variety of diameters for the parrot's foot. They should be roughened up with a file or rasp and made thinner in several spots. The two or three perches must be placed parallel to each other, not crosswise. Droppings should not fall on the lower perch. The top perch should be located so that the bird in an upright position has at least 1 cm. headroom. Furthermore, its tail feathers should not touch the wire when it bends forward. When sleeping, birds prefer to sit on an upper perch because this location gives them the greatest feeling of security. If the space beneath the cage roof is too small, the bird will still sit up there, but in a bent position. If the space is too great, the interiór of the cage is not being used fully. The lower perch is used mainly for reaching the feeding dishes, which are usually lower than the door. Another perch belongs outside, on top of the cage; if possible, it should extend out beyond one side. The parrot needs room for its tail

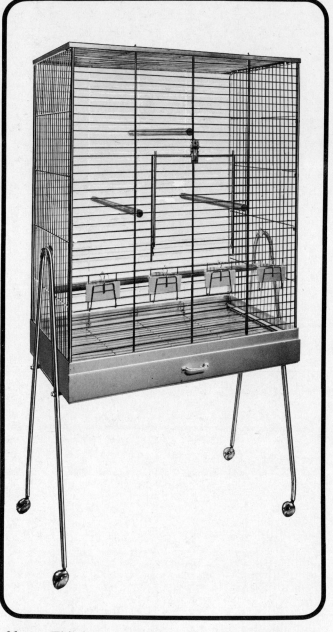

Above: This large cage (80 × 50 × 106 cm.) for one or two amazons has four dishes for a versatile feeding program. Food dispensers can be installed in place of the two outer dishes.

Left, above: The sight of an 18-month-old Yellow-crowned Amazon (*A. ochrocephala ochrocephala*) licking oatmeal off a spoon may be cute, but other feeding methods are preferable for hygienic reasons. Much of the food ends up on the floor after a short time; such liberal feeding is natural for an amazon.

Left, below: Hispaniolan Amazon (*A. ventralis*).

Blue-fronted Amazons (*A. aestiva*) in a wrought-iron parrot cage.

Above: A door that opens downward may be soiled by droppings.

Below: A bird may injure itself on protruding cage wires.

feathers. If it sits on the end of this perch, then its droppings will not fall on the cage wires or into the dishes.

3. DISHES AND DOOR Dishes for parrots must be fastened very securely. It must be impossible for the bird to push the dishes out from the inside and perhaps even squeeze through the opening itself. Upon removal of the dishes, it must be possible to close off the resultant openings with a fastening device. The openings for the dishes should not be below the door opening. If one wants to install an automatic food dispenser, it will have to be fastened to the wires above the dish with a clamp. It is best to ask for a demonstration of the fastening procedure when buying the food dispenser. R. Low writes that these food dispensers are not for real bird lovers. Whoever cares for an animal should take the time to feed it daily. Besides, the food supply can block up in the neck, and the bird then sits in front of the dish, unable to get to the food. On the bottom of the dish of the dispenser an unappetizing layer of dust forms. Therefore, the dispenser should be used only exceptionally, for a short period of time. Moreover, the typical commercial dispensers are easily pushed away by the amazons when they hang on the outside of the cage, and the contents are spilled all over the floor.

The door should close in a way that is parrot-proof. This is true if a human has to exert a certain force to open in. A bolt should not be within reach from inside. A door that opens downward ensures the least danger of injury to the bird. But it could be hit by droppings. This can be prevented by directing the bird in its choice of a perch; a natural branch fastened to the top on the appropriate side usually works. If the door is hinged on the side, one should watch for protruding wire ends. They are dangerous, but they can be bent away with pliers. Doors which are pulled up or hinged at the top must be fastened to be kept open, so that the bird cannot lock itself out. An excellent solution is the following: The entire front of the cage is hinged as a door, and in this is an

The designers of this parrot cage were really thinking! The wiring is horizontal all the way around, and the entire front can be opened and rotated 270 degrees. It can be fastened open by a latch at the rear. Chrome- or brass-plated wiring, measuring 45 x 45 x 75 cm. Two perches are supplied, but they should be placed in parallel.

additional, small door. Thus, the parrot can fly directly to its perch. Recalcitrant animals can be put back into the cage more easily, since the opening is so wide. A cage with an opening front is an added advantage during taming. An entrance perch can be fastened in the door opening to facilitate the parrot's getting in and out, at least in the beginning.

4. CAGE BOTTOM Most cages have a plastic base with a wire grate. The function of the latter is to keep the amazon from stepping in its own droppings on the floor, but some of the droppings always stick to the grate so it might as well be taken out right away. One good use for the wire grate is as a separator when two incompatible amazons which normally have their own cages must be in one cage for a short time during transport. For a long period, naturally, this is not a solution.

The plastic base gradually becomes worn by the sprinkled sand, and the material itself becomes brittle in time. When purchasing the cage one should ask whether the shop will be able to supply a replacement base should the first one break or become unusable. Cages that have a pull-out tray are more practical. It is easier to clean the floor without having to set the wire top aside. On the other hand, there is no possibility of putting only the top over a bird which does not return to the cage willingly.

5. LOCATION The stand offered with the cage is usually 50–60 cm. high. This is too low, because the parrot should be at eye level with the observer. It is disturbing to the amazon if one looks into the cage from above. Consider hanging the cage on a wall; this gives the animal cover on one side. The location should not be exposed to full sunlight. Drafts are to be avoided, as is the immediate proximity of a radiator. The room itself should receive sunlight once a day. Since amazons always want to be one of the party, it is recommended that space be reserved for the cage in several places throughout the house. In the appropriate rooms two hooks should be fastened to the wall, where the cage can be

Above: Parrot cage (68 × 70 × 100 cm.) with four dishes and a metal tray painted beige. Available either galvanized or brass-plated, with a stand. Large enough for two amazons, provided additional perches are installed.

Left, above: A parrot like this Yellow-crowned Amazon (*A. ochrocephala ochrocephala*), 3 years old, should be chained only during excursions outdoors, as on this walk through a corn field. As its wings have not been clipped, it uses them frequently in the house.

Left, below: Blue-cheeked Amazon (*A. dufresniana dufresniana*).

Blue-fronted Amazon (*A. aestiva*).

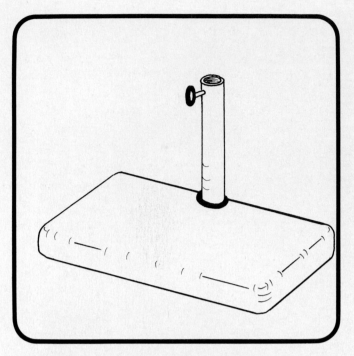

Above: Branches or an artificial climbing tree are secured in this stand by a thumbscrew.

Below: The stability of a stand may be enhanced by screwing it to a larger base.

hung as needed. This way, the amazon can be brought along, without one worrying that it will damage something with its beak. The kitchen and the bedroom are no place for an amazon; this must be mentioned to keep the reader from drawing the wrong conclusion. With a recently purchased animal, a certain reticence in this respect is normally exercised. However, as the years pass, one becomes more intimate with an amazon, but this should not be at the cost of hygiene.

Stand and Climbing Tree To keep an amazon on a parrot stand all day long, chained by one foot, is simply mistreatment of the animal. When a parrot stand is mentioned here, it must be understood that it is to be used in addition to the cage. The tray catches droppings and other debris produced by the amazon. Naturally, a single perch offers few climbing possibilities, so one should provide a climbing tree as well. This can easily be constructed by trimming branches to the desired size and then screwing or nailing them together. The whole is set into a Christmas-tree stand or an outdoor umbrella stand. First, the branches must be brushed while wet, so that neither dirt nor possible insecticides continue to adhere to them. In addition, the leaves should be checked for "little beasties" which are not wanted in the house. The branches should be arranged so that the amazon does not expel its droppings onto the lower ones. In actuality this can be difficult, because they always hit something. Another possibility is an artificial climbing tree; its design will allow the problem of the droppings to be taken into consideration. For the authors, a flat, ladderlike structure has proven itself. It is held vertical by a rectangular umbrella stand.

Bird Rooms A bird room must be heatable and should receive some sunlight daily. In winter, the photoperiod must be lengthened artificially to twelve hours, for which it is best to use "truelite" tubes. The light they produce approximates natural daylight. With a timer, they can be turned on at 4:00 AM, so the end

Above: This stand incorporates a tin plate 71 cm. in diameter and a heavy base. The chrome-plated arm ends in a wooden perch, to which two dishes are attached. This design suits those who like to use newspaper in the tray.

of the twelve-hour "day" will coincide with the time of sunset. Even at night, the room should not be pitch dark. If there is no light entering from outside, an 8-watt bulb should remain burning. H. Schnabl describes a complete lighting arrangement in *Die Voliere*, 1981/2.

A window allows direct contact with the outside air. A grating which can be set into the window opening as needed permits air flow without giving the birds an opportunity to get away. The interior furnishings must be such that neither they nor the parrots can be injured. If the heat source becomes so hot that the birds could burn their feet, it must be enclosed with a grating. The unpapered walls should be provided with a coating of whitewash (Aschenborn), with roofer's tin or Resopal (Pinter), or with a washable paint of the kind used for bathrooms. The floor must be such that it can be kept clean. It should be caulked and then covered with sand.

A. Gemein renovated a massive brick house for keeping parrots, covering the interior rooms with a layer of unpolluted earth from the forest, 30 cm. thick. On this he piled tree roots, rotted tree parts, and large, room-high tree trunks. Such bird rooms are optimal, but not everyone can recreate the primeval forest as

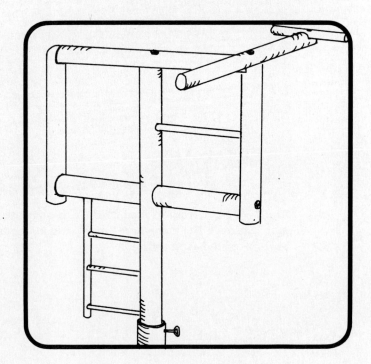

Right: An artificial climbing tree.

A pair of Blue-fronted Amazons (*A. aestiva*) set up
in an outdoor flight for breeding. A trash can has
been provided for nesting.

Yellow-naped Amazon (*A. ochrocephala auropalliata*) on a playground which has been furnished with a food dish, chewing toys, a ladder, and a swing.

perfectly as Gemein has described in his book. Anyone who lives in a rented dwelling must exercise restraint. The use of sand as a floor covering is not possible; one must compromise. Bird rooms can look very different, depending on circumstances. The comments in this book are intended only as examples; this is also true for the next section on aviaries.

Aviaries: *1. ROOM AVIARIES* When one keeps amazons, one would also like to observe them. This is not easily possible in the bird room described, because one must normally enter the room, thus intruding into the territory of the birds. (If the doings of the amazons can be observed through a glass door or a glass wall, this is naturally simpler. A. Gemein uses a video surveillance installation; other parrot lovers simply put an old easy chair in the bird room and let the animals get used to the observer.)

With a room aviary, one does not have these problems. The amazons are accustomed to more intensive contact with humans. They let themselves be observed unself-consciously, yet are among their own kind. One can order room aviaries, shipped unassembled, by mail order. Pet shops furnish room aviaries made to measure. These have wire on all sides. In practice, they are like large cages. If one would like to construct a room aviary, one can construct it in a corner of the room, thereby saving two sides. As material, one should use spot-welded, galvanized iron mesh, which is welded to a framework of square tubes (Pinter). For amazons, one should use a wire 2 mm. in diameter and a mesh size of 25 mm. The door should be at most 1 m. tall, so that the birds cannot easily get out when one enters the aviary. The floor should consist of sheet metal which is folded up 20 cm. on each side and then covered with sand. According to Pinter, the walls of the room should be covered with plywood paneling.

2. BALCONY AVIARIES Balcony aviaries are constructed in exactly the same way, being topped in addition with a wire roof and having an open passageway into the interior of the

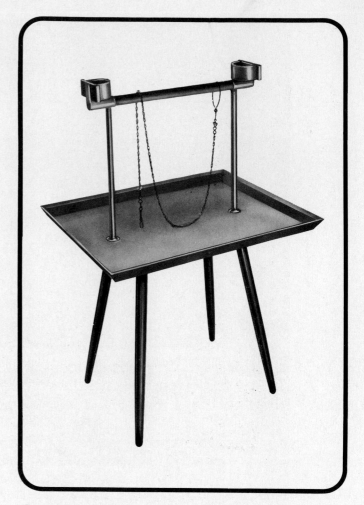

A parrot stand 98 cm. high, with a tray 60 x 44 cm.

40

The authors developed this parrot stand, which is easy to construct. Newspaper placed beneath will catch the droppings. An advantage of this stand is its low weight: when going to another room, it and the amazon are simply carried along. At bath time, the stand can just be put into the bathtub.

On its side, the stand has space for two amazons, so that each has its own perch. Even clipped birds have room to move away.

house, through which the parrots can enter the room aviary during bad weather. When one enters the balcony aviary through the door (1 m. high at most) for feeding or cleaning, added care is needed to keep one's wards from getting away. Security is offered only by a "lock" [a vestibule and a second door].

3. OUTDOOR AVIARIES It is not sufficient to set a wire-mesh structure on the bare ground. This is not recommended for hygienic reasons, because the excretions pollute the soil. Unwelcome visitors like mice, rats, cats, weasels, polecats, and other vermin can get in too easily. A foundation made of concrete or bricks will prevent this. In order to keep the mice from digging underneath, the foundation must extend into the ground for 50 cm., or even 1 m., according to Pinter. A concrete floor is safest, but wire mesh, set into the earth to a depth of 50 cm., then horizontally extended, will also keep the rodents out (Enehjelm). Wilker (in *AZN* 9/78) recommends putting in a horizontal layer of cinderblocks. He describes a foundation of edgingstones (99 x 8 x 30 cm.) which has the advantage of letting rain water drain through open side joints. One sees that there are no limits to the imagination of the aviary builder. Naturally, mice must also be prevented from above-the-ground access to food dishes and food remnants strewn about. A strip of small-mesh netting 20 cm. wide is placed around the aviary. Cats and owls can be kept out only by a double layer of mesh; but they haven't much chance with the amazons, as these birds know how to defend themselves.

The aviary requires a shelter room and a wire-glass shelter wall (Pinter). These are oriented toward the weather side, i.e., toward north or east. The shelter room must be well insulated and electrically heated. An infrared heater or two carbon-filament lamps, covered with wire mesh and coupled with a thermostat, will keep the temperature at a minimum of about 15 C. even in winter. In the shelter room, there should be a small vestibule, which serves as a lock. This is also where tools and

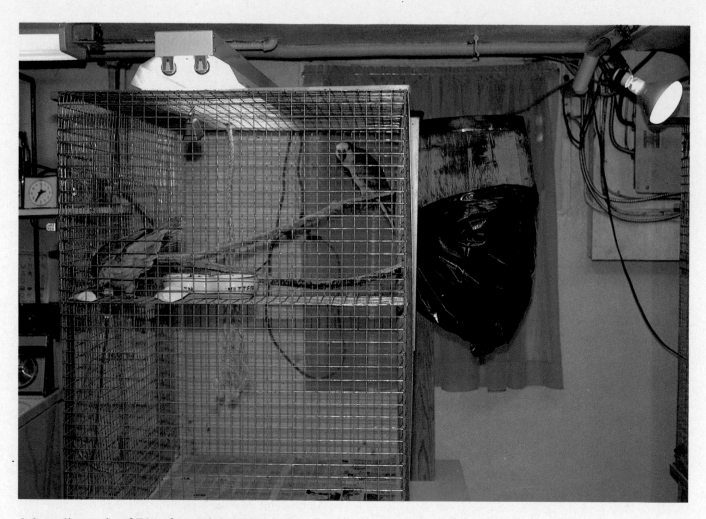

A breeding pair of Blue-fronted Amazons (*A. aestiva*). Note the wooden-keg nest attached outside the enclosure.

food can be stored. Through another door from the shelter room, one reaches the actual aviary. It is partially roofed with wire glass, so that the animals sitting outdoors do not have to retreat to the inside because of a rain shower. The wire mesh is galvanized, spot-welded iron mesh 2 mm. thick with a mesh size of 25 mm. or, as recommended by Gemein, so-called corrugated wire with a mesh size of 40 mm., which will withstand even the beaks of macaws and cockatoos. As protective paint for the wire, de Grahl recommends a bitumen lacquer which does not splinter off as easily as iron lacquer and has to be renewed only every two years.

The interior is furnished with climbing trees and perches. With sloping perches, amazons can get to the ground and up again without flying. Nest boxes should be offered both inside and outside the shelter. (If there are several amazons together, no breeding attempts should be made before the breeding pair is separated from the others.) Any plantings inside will soon be destroyed by the amazons; however, it is important that the aviary be surrounded by greenery. For breeding amazons especially, it is important that they can feel undisturbed and safe.

Yellow-naped Amazon (*A. ochrocephala auropalliata*), less than a year old.

Feeding

General Amazons in captivity depend entirely on what we offer them to eat. It should be understood that we should give them as large a selection as possible from which to choose. Seed and water alone are not sufficient. If an amazon stays alive despite such sparse meals, it demonstrates only that it can make do with a one-sided diet, if need be. Such a bird will hardly want to breed; that it will have little resistance against infections must be feared. A well-rounded diet, on the other hand, guarantees perfect plumage, in addition to sound health and well-being. Finally, even in the wild amazons do not restrict themselves to plundering only a wheat field on any given day, even though they would get filled there. Rather, they fly large distances to obtain a varied diet. They spend many hours searching for food. Nowhere else is it as easy as in cages or aviaries, of course. In nature they do not always find everything in large amounts, and there are always, at the same time, other hungry beaks in the same place. Eating is part of the battle for survival.

The beak is in constant action. We have to consider this when the amazons sit in our cages or aviaries. The need to gnaw persists, even though the necessary food can be eaten in a short time. One should unconditionally offer a selection of different kinds of foods, including nuts in their shells, if possible, so that the bird has at least some work to do. Eating should always be a pleasurable pastime. As far as the suitability of certain staples such as parrot food is concerned, different authors disagree. The following is intended to give the reader an overview of the possibilities, to instruct him without taking the decision away from him. How feeding methods have changed in the past hundred years has been described in a previous chapter.

Seed Amazons like to eat white, striped, or black sunflower seeds best of all. Which color or size they prefer is variable; one should expect that an amazon which is used to white sunflower seeds will turn down the striped ones. The sizes of the kernels differ. If the dish is filled with large, white seeds, the amazon will have less food substance than with small ones, for most is air and hull. This means more frequent refills. One should check occasionally how much is inside a sunflower seed; after all, only the inner part is eaten. One can conduct a taste test at the same time. If the kernel tastes bad, it is not all right for the amazon either. These so-called oil seeds (think of the margarine which is manufactured from them) are not suitable as the birds' sole food. They should constitute no more than 60% of the diet. Otherwise, the diet would be too one-sided, since sunflower seeds contain so much fat. (According to Pinter, sunflower kernels contain 54.3% raw fat, 20.4% raw protein, 6.0% carbohydrates, 4.1% fiber, 2.7% ash (minerals), and 12.5% water.) Therefore, one also should feed hulled oats, corn, wheat, and millet spray. Basically, amazons do not care for the very small seeds, but if they can be made to accept canary seed, it is all for the best. These seeds contain a higher proportion of carbohydrate (60–70%), only about 5% raw fat, and are not very rich in protein (10–15%).

Protein, however, is important for the formation of body substance. It builds muscle, organ tissue, feathers, and horn. It is the peas in the seed mixture which contain more than 30% raw protein (raw protein: the body cannot use all of it, only about half). To vary the menu of the amazon as much as possible, one may also offer squash seeds, hemp, and peanuts, but in small amounts, because these too contain fat. Peanuts in their shells are especially relished, because they can be cracked. There is a difference between feed peanuts (available in pet shops) and table peanuts (available in groceries). The first taste awful on our tongues because they have not been roasted. Amazons eat them unhesitatingly. However, R. Low writes that only those peanuts intended for human consumption should be fed (in their shells), because with the others a fungus (*Aspergillus flavus*) has been spread on occasion; it is not known to what extent this observation, made in England, is applicable to our situation. There is one thing that we must never do: feed salted peanuts. Nuts—such as hazelnuts, beechnuts, walnuts, brazil nuts, edible and wild chestnuts, acorns and pine nuts, some of which have to be cracked for the amazons— complement the seed offering.

In pet shops one can buy prepackaged foods for amazons (parrot food). These are available in packages of 1 kg., bags of 5 kg., or plastic bags. The last are usually somewhat cheaper, because the shop has made the mixture for its own use. On the other hand, many products have wood for gnawing added, which increases its usefulness. Of importance in prepackaged food is the manufacturing date which is stamped onto the box. The food should be transferred to a glass container immediately; at the same time one can check to see whether it is still fresh. Rancid food is evident from the smell. Sometimes there are small grubs, worms, or insect larvae on the inside of the carton; this is cause for complaint. In addition, the seed should not be dusty. If necessary, it can be washed quickly and dried. The new harvest always comes toward the end of the year. But first the old stock must be sold. Between the harvest of the sunflower seed and its distribution to the user, many months, even years, can pass (Heidenreich).

Not all the seeds contained in the parrot mix will be eaten. One should not make the amazons wait for a refill until the last grain of wheat has been eaten. The uneaten food should be removed together with the hulls of the other seeds. By offering different seeds separately, one can find out which foods are most worthwhile and compose one's own mixture accordingly. R. Low recommends a separate dish for each kind of seed. In most cages there are no provisions for this. However, one can fasten other dishes with wire on the right and the left, into which (for instance) very small seeds can be put. These must not be mixed with sunflower seeds because they literally sink to the bottom.

Sprouts Sprouted seed is a valuable supplementary food, especially in winter, when no fresh greens can be obtained from the garden. The process of sprouting unlocks some nutrients in the seed, develops vitamins (e.g., vitamin E), and makes all its components more easily digestible. In principle, sprouting is very simple: The desired quantity (for one amazon, one tablespoon of seed is sufficient) is first washed well, then soaked for twenty-four hours in water. After that, the seed is rinsed in a sieve and set into a shallow dish with little water, which is covered with a glass and set into a warm (20 C.), well-lighted spot. After another twenty-four hours, the swollen seeds are ready to be fed, or one can wait another day until the sprouts have broken through. Before feeding, the seeds should be rinsed once more.

It goes without saying that sprouted seed should be offered in a separate dish. Uneaten leftovers should be removed soon, as sprouts spoil quickly. They can get moldy or smell rotten and must then be thrown out. If the dish is fastened upside down, with its bottom up, one can put a shallow layer of sprouts on it. These will dry out in time and will be less likely to rot or turn sour than when they are heaped inside the dish. If sprouting is done often, one will develop one's own methods. Many bird keepers sprout the different kinds of seeds separately, because they all have a different germination period. Should the first attempts at sprouting be unsuccessful, one should not give up. Sometimes the fault lies with the seeds themselves, having been stored so long that they have lost their ability to germinate. In health-food stores and in mail-order catalogs there are sprouting apparatuses with which sprouts for human use (e.g., wheat sprouts) can be grown. In addition, in health-food stores, sprouting seeds can be bought which will be a hundred percent successful. If the amazons have no appetite for

Above: Properly, a singly kept amazon, such as this Yellow-crowned Amazon (*A. ochrocephala ochrocephala*), should be taken along at every opportunity. During vacations it should not be given to someone else to take care of; instead, it should come along on the trip. Animals able to fly should be kept on a parrot chain.

Below: Having a drink while on the road.

sprouts despite all of this, one can safely eat them oneself.

Half-ripe Seed   Amazons like to eat wheat and oats in the half-ripe, milky state. Here, one gives the bird the whole ear, which it will hold in its foot and tear apart. Even more popular is a half-ripe ear of corn, shucked (be careful of lice!), cut into portions about 3 cm. long, and put into a dish. The whole ear can also be fastened to the cage. But if several amazons are kept, this can easily lead to fighting; therefore, cutting it up is better. Ears of corn can be fed as long as there are still some soft kernels. Fully ripe ears with hard kernels are picked apart more than eaten. Freezing a supply is another possibility.

Fruits and Greens   As a source of vitamins, fruit is indispensible in the care of parrots. Cut-up apples, pears, plums, peaches, bananas, oranges, tangerines, clementines, satsumas, cherries, grapes, unsulfurized raisins, figs, and all the berries in the garden can be offered. Whether the amazon will eat everything is a different question. Sweet fruits are preferred to acid ones, dry surfaces to wet ones. Once a particular flavor has been enjoyed, the amazon will eat that fruit again and again. It is best to show the amazon how it's done. One gives it some while eating some oneself. For single tame birds, this is always the best method to use to introduce a new fruit. In a group of amazons, there is always a food taster, i.e., an amazon that will be the first to take something new in its beak and crush it. The others will learn from it, sometimes even taking the pieces of fruit from its beak, after which they will accept the unusual food. Apple seeds and the inside of peach, plum, and cherry pits contain prussic acid, a poison. Ingested in large amounts, it is harmful; a single fruit, or its pit, is acceptable. Delpy writes (in *AZN* 1978) of instances of prussic acid poisoning in parrots, although rarely with a fatal outcome. He goes on to warn against canned fruit and frozen fruit. Canned fruit contains no vitamins, for it was usually harvested when still unripe. In

Double Yellow-headed Amazon (*A. ochrocephala oratrix*).

addition, there may be harmful substances from the cans.

All kinds of vegetables can also be fed: carrots contain valuable carotene, a precursor of vitamin A. Tomatoes, cucumbers, salsify, melons, celery, beets, spinach, and lettuce (unsprayed!) will be eaten. Of course, all must be impeccable produce which was first washed (and dried). One should feed only what one would be prepared to eat oneself, no kitchen parings. The opinions about the dangers of vegetables are divided: Aschenborn warns against all kinds of cabbage. Pinter recommends brussels sprouts and savoy cabbage; P. Deimer, kohlrabi. Fischer is against cabbage and legumes.

The greatest danger to the amazon is the chemical treatment of fruit and vegetables. Strongly sprayed apples should not only be washed, but also peeled. Orange rinds which have been waxed should not be given either. Just compare the body weight of an amazon with that of a human being: 500 g. vs. 50 kg. A human is, therefore, at least 100 times heavier. A man can tolerate substances which endanger his health better than a bird can. To return to the example of apple seeds containing prussic acid: If we eat an apple, core and all, it does not bother us. However, if an amazon picks out all the seeds in an apple, it could be dangerous. It is better not to permit the opportunity.

The following wild berries should be mentioned as appropriate fare: rose hips, rowan berry (fruit of the mountain ash), hawthorn berry, and elderberry. Greens like dandelions, chickweed, plantain, and parsley would also be healthful, but many amazons simply shake their heads when such herbs are placed before them. Or they pull on them briefly and then drop them. More appealing to gnawing hookbills are all the parts of a tree branch: buds, blossoms, small leaves, and bark. These trees should be mentioned: fruit trees, willows, maple, lime, oak, alder, poplar, birch, beech, and mountain ash. Of the bushes, those recommended are hazel, lilac, and elder. When collecting food or gnawing material outdoors, three things must be considered: Has it been treated with chemical sprays? Is it polluted with car exhaust

fumes and street dust? Is it permissible to remove these plants? (for instance, the pussy willow is protected [in Germany] as being the primary food of bees).

Animal Food As previously described, proteins are immensely important for the formation of the body's own proteins. With regular, supplementary protein foods, the amazon will grow faultless plumage. The production of feathers especially requires a constant supply of protein. Dr. M. Heidenreich (in *Die Voliere* 1981/2) writes that seedeaters are not exclusively vegetarians. Worms and all stages of insects are taken in considerable quantity. He developed a diet supplement which contains animal fats and proteins in addition to carbohydrates, minerals, trace elements, and vitamins. These are slightly damp, brownish-red crumbs whose consistency is reminiscent of fine potting soil. This "vital concentrate" is more readily accepted by parrots than raw meat.

Very much appreciated as a diet supplement is the Complete Honey Food Type III (Brown) of the firm of Claus, in Limburgerhof. This special mix is made primarily for insect-eating birds, but is also suitable for parrots. Another complementary food are the Pellets manufactured by Claus which contain all essential components in balanced form. Amazons could be fed exclusively with this "complete parrot food," but this should not be done in preference to a wide range of basic foods.

Chopped, hard-boiled chicken eggs or a piece of breakfast egg, together with the shell, will also serve to fill the need for protein, even though the nutritive value of cooked (i.e., coagulated) egg white is not as high as that of raw egg white.

Raw, aged beef in the form of tartare can also be fed. One can serve small balls 1 cm. in diameter which have been warmed in the hand. Perhaps it can be mixed with soaked zwieback. After the meal, all leftovers should be removed. Once an amazon has become accustomed to the tartare, it enjoys it very much. A particularly suspicious amazon which flung the tartare away

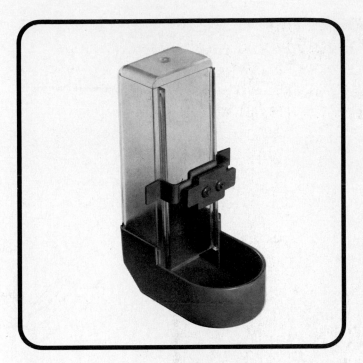

Above: A clamp fastens this food dispenser to the cage wires.

Below: Feeder with two dishes and a clamp. A similar model is designed for installation in cages.

for weeks was finally able to be trained to accept this supplementary food by an unusual method: the tartare-zwieback mixture was first chewed in the mouth and then fed by hand to the bird. A condition is that the keeper not have a cold or something similar which could be transmitted with the saliva. The normal bacterial flora of the mouth are not harmful. In no circumstances should anyone feed from his mouth to the beak, because in this case the human might become infected. Besides, the method described should be used only as an extraordinary measure to accustom the animal to the tartare, not as a customary procedure. De Grahl and Pinter consider raw meat to be unhealthy; this is mentioned for the sake of completeness and will be considered further in the following section.

Human Food With the aforementioned breakfast egg we have already touched on this controversial topic: foods as prepared for human consumption. In the literature of the past, they were proscribed; according to newer reports, they are perfectly acceptable as dietary supplements. Aschenborn considers them harmless, unless they are strongly salted or seasoned. Delpy, on the other hand, warns against bread and butter, fats in general, cooking salt, coffee, and alcohol. He considers hard rolls with cottage cheese and honey, soaked in milk, commendable. Pinter represents the view that the majority of human foods will be tolerated in small amounts by the parrots. Cooked potatoes, pasta, bread and butter, and cake in small amounts are permitted. Cheese might cause an obstruction of the crop if it is eaten in too large amounts. Meat should be avoided. Yet other authors consider meat harmless or even an important protein factor. R. Low, for instance, writes that there is nothing better for an amazon than a chicken bone with some meat left on it. She means a roasted chicken. If not given in excess, human foods are said to be harmless and to increase the diversity of the feeding plan. During the Second World War, when no seed could be obtained in England, many parrots had to

survive almost exclusively on human food. P. Deimer too mentions cooked or raw, seasoned meat as supplementary food—in small amounts, of course—and cites the fact that amazons in the care of one keeper searched the ground in the aviary for worms during the course of one breeding attempt.

In our opinion, one should in the first place establish a well-balanced bird diet consisting of seeds, fruit, vegetables, and greens. In addition, human foods may be offered: zwieback, old rolls or white bread, flatbread (all spread with some honey); cooked potatoes, pasta, rice; hard-boiled eggs; steak tartare; cooked soup-, chop-, or chicken bones; and all kinds of noncarbonated fruit juices, not instead of drinking water, but in addition. Alcohol is prohibited. It is said that parrots become unpleasant after imbibing alcohol. Besides, it is a mischievous abuse. During parties, one must watch and make sure that no one takes the opportunity to feed the amazons inappropriately or gives them something

unsuitable to drink. Coffee is also unnecessary. Black tea—like all other kinds of tea—can be given according to the instructions of the veterinarian, in the treatment of diarrhea, for instance. For a change, corn-meal gruel can be fed. (Cook the corn meal in water for ten minutes, constantly stirring it, then let it cool.) Finally, baby cereals are a possible dietary supplement, especially for young amazons. These baby cereals are available in several varieties.

Vitamins, Minerals, and Trace Elements
The foods listed so far contain everything the amazon needs by way of vitamins, minerals, and trace elements. To make absolutely certain that the amazon lacks nothing, one can purchase a vitamin preparation in the pet shop. Available as a powder or a liquid, such preparations are best offered in the drinking water. If the amazon rejects this because of the taste, the vitamins can be mixed with soft, mushy foods. One can also buy a multivitamin

Facing page: Tame Blue-fronted Amazon (*A. aestiva*) in Salta, Argentina.

Above: Red-lored Amazon (*A. autumnalis autumnalis*).

preparation for small children (in bottles or tubes) at the pharmacy and give this in minute amounts. But be careful: the vitamins A, D, E, and K are fat soluble, and excessive dosages can be harmful (hypervitaminosis). The other vitamins, e.g., the vitamin-B complex and vitamin C, are water soluble and, in the case of excessive dosage, are excreted, unused, by the body. Be careful, then, with the dosage!

Mineral substances (sodium, phosphorus, calcium) and trace elements (iron, copper, zinc, potassium) are obtained by the amazon from its food and additionally from bird gravel, special mineral blocks, cuttlebone, ground egg shells, or oyster shell. One might ask where the amazon obtains all these materials in nature. It goes to the *colpa*, as J. Reichholf describes in *Sielmanns Tierwelt*, 3/81: "The *colpa* is something like a pharmacy or a fountain of life, where the animals find trace elements and minerals. Thus, the *colpa*, such as this clay wall, becomes a meeting place for the animals, where they satisfy their requirements for survival. These substances are in short supply because, far and wide, numerous plants filter them from the water."

Mineral blocks (beak conditioners) are more or less hard. The beak of the amazon demands very resistant material, otherwise it will make short shrift of them. Of importance also is a very strong wire hanger which is fastened deep in the stone, because this is where the amazon begins to gnaw, especially when the bird is hanging on the outside of the cage. With an experienced amazon, it takes less than ten minutes until a new, soft block drops to the bottom of the cage.

Drinking Water Water need not be boiled, except for sick animals, but it should always be fresh and clean. Bottled drinking water is not always as fresh as tap water. Enehjelm recommends tap water which has been permitted to stand for a while. For recently imported birds, P. Deimer recommends only boiled, lukewarm water.

Again and again, the amazon will pollute its water. First it drops food into it, then small pieces of gnawed wood or shreds of paper. Even shells, pebbles, and other gnawable material is likely to be thrown into the dish by the amazon. Therefore, the water must be replaced several times daily. Under no circumstances should it be possible for droppings to fall into the dish. If this is noticed, a Plexiglas cover must be installed. The water dishes must be thoroughly cleaned daily with a brush reserved especially for this use. Depending on the degree of hardness of the water, a chalky deposit will form on their corners and edges. This may be removed with a scouring agent, but this will damage the plastic surface. After about a year's use, a plastic dish can no longer be cleaned enough to look attractive and must be replaced; or it can be switched with the seed dish. In brown dishes the dirt is not as obvious as in white ones, but even so, scratches appear in the plastic surface after repeated scrubbing, into which dirt particles can settle. A dish should be clean enough that the bird keeper himself could eat or drink from it.

The half-round mineral block is firm enough, but the soft wires break too soon; the other has a strong fastener, but the brittle chalk is quickly destroyed by amazons.

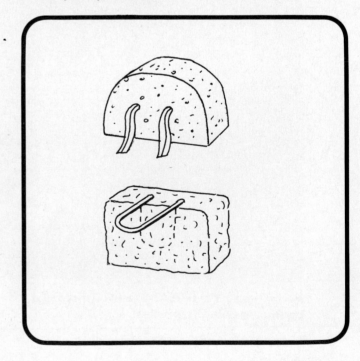

52

Care

Cleanliness of the Animal What kind of care does an amazon require? First, one has to see to the cleanliness of bird and cage. The bird itself should be showered at least once per week; Pinter even recommends a daily shower. This can be done with the help of a plant mister or with a hand-held shower attachment in the bathroom. Depending on the degree of tameness, one sprays the bird in its cage or while it is sitting on the hand. The water should be warm, but not hot. Care is required with small water heaters which do not maintain a constant water temperature. The fine mister does not beat on the plumage as hard as the bathroom shower. The spray of the shower can be directed upward, however, and the falling drops can rain on the amazon. As always, careful attention is necessary; one should stop immediately if the bird reacts defensively. A shower should be a pleasure for the amazon, not a punishment. If the bather remains sitting with shivering wings and its head thrown back, it is not enjoying the procedure. On the other hand, if it spreads its wings, makes wiping movements with its head, fans out its tail feathers, and utters little cries of pleasure, it obviously enjoys the bath. The bird does not have to be dripping wet each time. A brief shower, during which the water rolls off the feathers, is sufficient. In this instance, it will not be necessary to dry the bird. Tame amazons willingly accept all of this.

In the wild, however, many amazons avoid foggy areas and drenching rains, choosing instead dry routes for their flights (Forshaw). But with respect to care in captivity, the following is valid: If the shower is timed for the morning, the amazons have the rest of the day to dry and groom their feathers. In any case, they should go to sleep dry in the evening. Of course, they have to be protected against drafts especially, and it is good if during the drying period they can choose for themselves between sunlight and shade. Occasionally, amazons can be put out in their cages into a warm summer rain. In an aviary they will avail themselves of this opportunity anyway. If there is no rain for a long time, aviary amazons can be sprayed with a garden hose. If the feet of the amazon are dirty, the bird should be taken to a sink and its feet held under a warm stream of water. If one holds each foot with one hand, he or she will not be bitten by an intractable amazon, because one's hands are protected by the water. Frequently the bird will snap at the faucet with its beak. It is very important that its feet be kept clean; otherwise, bacteria can be transmitted.

Cleaning the Cage Where there are dirty toes, there are usually dirty perches. These too need to be cleaned immediately. Besides droppings, perches usually become soiled by pieces of food which are rubbed from the beak onto the perches. Regular cleaning is recommended, i.e., a weekly brushing with a hot soapy solution. Every morning the droppings from the night should be cleaned from the floor of the cage. Either remove a layer of paper from the cage floor, or sprinkle the little heap of droppings with bird sand and remove it with a small shovel. If one wants to clean the cage daily—and this should be done for the sake of the animal—putting several layers of newspaper on the bottom is recommended. These can be removed one by one, together with the droppings of the previous night, until gradually the paper is all used up. If we forego the use of bird sand on the cage floor, it must be offered elsewhere—for instance, sprinkled on the food. Seedeaters need sand in the gizzard for grinding seeds. The Duke of Bedford wrote that if we use bird sand on the floor of the cage, we should not use it as sparingly as if it were gold dust. After all, bird sand is not expensive. For parrots, one can

Yellow-crowned Amazon (*A. ochrocephala ochrocephala*) preening its wing feathers.

Double Yellow-headed Amazon (*A. ochrocephala oratrix*) responding to a spray bath with delight.

even use cat litter. Kaeding writes, "Let us stay with the old-fashioned, fresh sand daily" (*AZN* 8/80). The use of newspaper is to be rejected, according to him, because of the printers' ink contained in it and because the parrot rips the paper. Printers' inks containing lacquer, white lead, and lithopone (a mixture of zinc sulfide and barium sulfate) could in theory be detrimental to the health of the parrot. However, the bird does not swallow the torn paper, at most touching it with its tongue—and what else does the tongue touch when it picks up seed? Be that as it may, whoever uses unprinted sheets instead of newspaper and then covers them with bird sand is certainly doing his best. We go along with R. Low, who also puts newspapers on the cage floor and changes them daily. She writes that ripping newspaper is not harmful but serves to entertain the parrot. However, this is not the best pastime, because if the paper is soiled with droppings, the amazon really should not play with it. Therefore, if it should get the idea to pull up the whole layer of papers, we should stop this immediately by putting in the wire grate. By the way, this is one of the few instances in which the grate can be useful.

With a stack of paper, the top sheet can be removed daily.

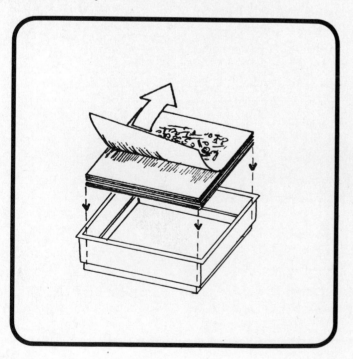

Once a month the cage should be thoroughly cleaned, the tray rinsed out with hot water, the wires brushed and rubbed dry. A careful cleansing with common detergents, followed by a rinse with (boiling) hot water, is normally sufficient. Disinfectants are used mainly in the quarantine area and when illness is suspected or confirmed. With newly acquired birds, one will want to disinfect more frequently. Solutions of formaldehyde should be used sparingly, since they are said to have carcinogenic effects (for the human who uses them for cleaning). The instructions for dilution must be exactly followed. The climbing tree or ladder must also be cleaned regularly or, better yet, replaced. After four weeks the amazon will have gnawed off the bark and the tree will no longer be of interest. The same is true of the climbing ladder: the amazon will have gnawed the wood in several places, but it won't be as much fun as it used to be. The ladder must be rebuilt or furnished with new twigs, which will offer the beak of the amazon new points of attack. In aviaries, the sand or grass should be raked well weekly (Bielfeld). At longer intervals, the floor covering should be completely replaced. If there is no concrete underneath, but natural earth, this must be turned over twice annually to the depth of a spade and renewed.

The room in which the amazon is kept should be well ventilated. As de Grahl mentions, parrots need air rich in oxygen. Above all, the amazon should not be sentenced to become a passive smoker! While the room is aired out, the amazon should not be exposed to drafts, because this will lead to colds even in acclimated amazons. However, a change of temperature, such as a move from a cooler to a warmer place, is not harmful to the bird. When travelling by car, one must be sure that vents and air conditioners do not cause a draft.

Cage: Covered or Not? Whether the cage should be covered at night or not cannot be answered categorically. One can be of two minds about this. In favor of a cover are the following: Amazons are cavity breeders, so they feel at ease in a completely enclosed space. In a

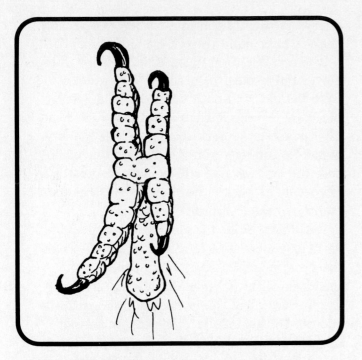

Above: The right foot of an amazon. The longer outer toes have longer claws.

Below: The claw to the left is not too long. If one cuts off the tip because it scratches, the desired result will be only temporary. With every cut, growth is activated, and the tip grows back more rapidly. The claw on the right is really too long. It must be shortened to normal length before the bird catches it and breaks or tears it off.

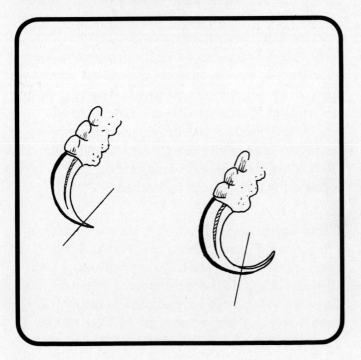

covered cage, amazons are protected from drafts. Therefore, if they are accustomed to a cover, they will not be afraid of it. Against covering are the following arguments: Amazons will be isolated from the family life in the evening. They will go to sleep even without a cover if they get tired. Amazons need much oxygen. If they are covered only when we ourselves go to bed, it is dark anyway. What good does the cover do?

One should find out by observation what the amazon prefers. It must be considered a sign of discomfort if the bird continues to move back and forth on its perch, climbs diagonally through the cage, and finds no rest. It is considered a sign of well-being if the amazon rests on one foot and hides its head in the feathers of its back, uttering small clucking sounds. Perhaps it will rub its lower mandible on the horny edges of its upper mandible. Some amazons which have been in captivity for a longer time have been observed sleeping with their heads toward the front.

Handling Wild Amazons Before claw, beak, and wing-feather trimming is discussed in the following paragraphs, the handling of wild amazons should be described here. This also applies to tame amazons that let themselves be petted but not forcibly held. One needs a thick towel, wood to bite on (e.g., a perch), a helper, and a steady hand. The towel is thrown over the bird when it sits on a level surface, such as a chair or a table. It should be grasped firmly and wrapped up. It is important that both wings be positioned correctly alongside the body. Then the amazon is put on the table, where its head is freed first. In this stressful situation, its requirements for oxygen are increased, and it must be able to breathe unobstructedly. The beak may bite the round wood. With it, the head of the bird (the animal lies on its back) is gently pushed downward onto the tabletop. Other objects can also be used to occupy the beak. It is likely that the amazon will free itself from its wrappings and, if flighted, may do damage to the room or injury to itself during an escape attempt. Such

Above: This Yellow-crowned Amazon (*A. ochrocephala ochrocephala*) is used to being chained. The leash of artificial fibers is only a slight hindrance in the course of excursions outdoors.

Below: Affixing the leg ring for the leash is no trouble if the amazon is tame.

escapades usually end in a corner, where the cloth is once more thrown over the bird.

It is possible to grab the amazon with thick gloves but it must be grabbed very quickly from behind, and both wings be held against the body to keep it from fluttering. One hand must enclose the neck so tightly that the lower mandible cannot reach the fingers, but making sure the amazon will still be able to breathe. However, its neck is nowhere as thick as the feathers make it appear.

With more skill, the amazon can be held without gloves. The left hand grasps it around the neck, pushing down against the upper mandible with the index finger and arresting the movement of the lower mandible with the thumb. In this manner, the amazon cannot open its beak and bite. However, care must be taken that the nostrils remain free so that the bird can breathe. Since holding is performed with the left hand, the right is free for the actual "operation," such as beak trimming. If the amazon is to become hand-tame but this is not yet accomplished, the towel method should be used. Otherwise, it may become afraid of hands. Many amazons have unpleasant memories of gloves from their quarantine period. If a towel is used, the amazon will at most be afraid of the towel in the future, but not of the human hand.

It is sometimes recommended that unpleasant tasks be done by a stranger, to keep the amazon from losing its trust in its keeper. However, our experience is that an amazon, once it has come to trust its keeper, will not resent any chore, even if it should hurt occasionally. In addition, small-animal veterinarians and pet shops are more than willing to assist with the necessary operations. With some patience and understanding, the following operations can be learned.

Claw Trimming Normally, claw trimming is unnecessary because the claws wear down by themselves. If they are cut, they will grow back all the quicker. It is true that once you begin to cut, you will always have to cut. Basically, one should refrain from attempting to regulate the growth of the claws with a clipper. If this

Green-cheeked Amazon (*A. viridigenalis*).

section mentions clipping claws at all, it is only because cage birds occasionally show abnormal growth of the claws. Of course, this differs from case to case. If one notices that the amazon cannot grip well, walks badly, and cannot move unimpeded along the cage wires because overly long claws keep getting caught, one should decide to cut the claws. A tame amazon will permit its claws to be clipped while sitting on the left hand of the keeper, conversing intimately with him. It will barely notice when from time to time a claw tip is shortened with the nail clipper.

It is best to work with a nail clipper meant for the human foot. Scissors are not suitable because the claw will twist during cutting. A claw clipper for dogs or a wire cutter with sharp edges are also suitable tools.

With untame amazons, a helper will be needed to hold the animal still (see the section on handling). With the left hand, one grasps a foot, and with thumb and index finger holds the toe which is to be worked on. Of course, one must not cut into the blood vessels which run through the claws. In pale horn, one can see them shine through. In dark horn, it may be possible to see them when the claw is held in front of a bright light source. The site of the cut should lie 2 mm. from the end of the blood vessel. Cutting through the horny substance without circulation is as painless for the birds as the cutting of fingernails is for us. Only if the blood vessels are injured, which should never happen, is this very painful for the amazon, even though it is not dangerous. In the case of such bleeding, the wound should be patted with absorbent cotton. In an emergency, cotton rinsed in salt water will do. Often such patting will not be possible, because the amazon will do anything in its power to prevent anyone from touching the injured foot. Now the wound must be observed. As a rule, the bleeding will stop by itself after a short time. If drops still form after an hour, a veterinarian must be consulted. It is important that the bird be immobilized. If the amazon bangs the claw against anything, it easily may begin to bleed again. This later bleeding will

Above: Drawing of a normal wing.

Below: If a bird flaps a lot during transport and quarantine and damages its clipped flights on cage wires, it is possible that the site of growth may be destroyed and the wing feathers will not grow in again. For the rest of its life the bird will be unable to fly and to hold its own among flighted conspecifics.

stop quickly because of the clotting ability of the blood. It is advisable that on one day only one foot be treated. Two weeks later, the other can be trimmed. The bird can thus adapt gradually. After a claw trimming, it will pull up the treated foot and stand on the other. The bird has become so accustomed to the long claws that sitting with normal claws seems strange.

The claws can also be trimmed another way: While the amazon is sitting in its cage, one notices a foot on the wire—perhaps in play. One takes the nail clipper and shortens the claws. If this disturbs the amazon to the extent that it may damage its feathers, one should release the foot immediately, and then consider trying one of the methods described previously.

Trimming the Beak   A too-long upper mandible interferes with an amazon's feeding and with its preening. One may trim the beak as one does the claws, but here too care must be taken because the upper part is hollow and has blood circulation. Nor must the tongue be injured. The amazon should be held as described earlier, and be biting on a round stick. The tip of the beak is then trimmed with a nail clipper, claw clipper, or wire cutter with sharp edges. Sometimes the amazon will grab the clipper with its beak. In this instance, the bird should quickly be held firm and the clipper carefully brought to a correct position before cutting. With tame amazons, as mentioned, it may be possible to hold the beak closed if one wishes to trim it. Since the upper mandible is longer and protrudes over the lower mandible, cutting a closed beak is easily accomplished. It is quite normal for flakes to come off the upper mandible occasionally. It happens especially during trimming that the outer layers become loose. These white flakes can be scratched off with a fingernail or filed off. These layers form because the beak grows from the inside outward.

Normally the lower mandible is never too long, since the amazon files it daily. After each meal the parrot sharpens it against the ridges on the upper mandible. If it is trimmed, its edge will be dull, and for a time the animal will

Above: Outline of the wing to show the position of the bones. From left to right: tip of the humerus; the radius above the ulna; the two small carpal bones; the carpometacarpus with the alula digit above; and finally, the two phalanges of the major digit with the minor digit below.

Below: A widely practiced method involves clipping all the primaries.

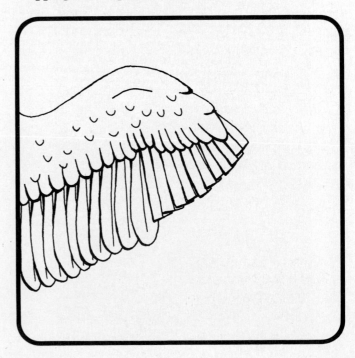

61

Above: Mealy Amazon *(A. farinosa).*
The upper mandible should be allowed to become no longer than this.

Below: Black-billed Amazon *(A. agilis).*
Quarantine always causes considerable physical and emotion stress.

no longer be able to crack seed. Sometimes it appears that the lower mandible is too long, and one thinks that the amazon can no longer close its beak correctly. The tongue is visible from the side. This is because part of the upper mandible has broken off, perhaps because of excessive climbing on the cage wires. Trimming the lower mandible would be wrong; it would not enable the animal to close its beak. The situation is different with obvious deformations of the beak, in which case a veterinarian must be consulted. The more climbing and gnawing possibilities the amazon has at its disposal, the fewer will be the worries about excessively long horny parts. For wearing down the claws, Pinter recommends square, slightly rounded perches.

Wing Clipping Before the wing feathers are clipped, each amazon keeper should consider whether this is really necessary. Wearing a parrot chain will prevent flight during times when the animal is taken outside. Thus the bird could be permitted to fly through the house, but it would be put on a chain to go outside. Otherwise, wing trimming will be necessary at intervals of six to twelve months. The clipping should be done so that it is not possible to see that the wings have been clipped when they lay flat against the parrot's body. The bird's back should remain covered. How this is possible when the wings are clipped becomes clear when one considers the construction of the wings and how they are artfully folded and laid against the body. One distinguishes between primary and secondary flight feathers, depending on which part of the wing the feathers grow from. When the wing is closed, the ten primaries lie below the ten secondaries, and, in amazons, only their tips are visible. When the bird lets its wings droop, to dry its feathers after a shower, for instance, the primaries become visible from the side. They are longer, and their inner vanes are black.

Of course, only the feathers are clipped, not the skin or the bones of the wing. One can easily imagine what the latter look like if one pictures the wing of a roasted chicken. The

Yellow-crowned Amazons: *A. ochrocephala panamensis*, 12 years old, and *A. ochrocephala oratrix*, 1 year old.

wing has the shape of a *Z*. The three parts represent upper arm, lower arm, and hand. In birds the "hand" has changed, and small bones only suggest three fingers. When clipping the outermost primaries, one must never cut the bird's hand. Also to be avoided is cutting a blood feather, i.e., a feather which is still growing, so the quill still has some blood circulation. Cutting one of these is painful to the animal and leads to a loss of blood.

It is best to clip the feathers after the molt, when they have reached their full length. An amazon can cover great distances when only two thirds of its wing feathers have grown in again. Even with only two primaries and a great deal of effort, it can accomplish a short flight of several meters. Thus there is a point in time when the keeper does not suspect his charge of being able to fly yet, but the bird suddenly and successfully tries to get away. So, foresight is necessary, and only after another trimming can the amazon be permitted outside once more. The same number of feathers should be removed right and left, so that the animal can get to the floor, under control, during an "emergency landing." With one-sided clipping, the animal loses its balance. The long, narrow primaries have the greatest carrying power. If they are cut (a few centimeters from the point where they are attached), the amazon will no longer be able to fly upwards, but at most horizontally for a short distance. The same result is achieved by cutting feathers from the middle of the wing, leaving at least the outermost three primaries in place. When the wing is closed, no cut feather stumps will be visible. Another way to diminish the carrying power of the wings is to clip every other feather. Usually, this method is almost undetectable. However, for a strong bird which is used to flight, this is not enough clipping. One must then trim the vanes of the remaining primaries. This will further reduce flying ability without causing appearance to suffer too much. It is often amazing how far a trimmed bird can fly if it is in good condition.

The greatest difficulty is not in isolating the feathers which are to be trimmed, but in

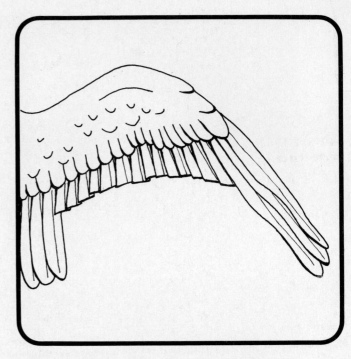

Above: Clipping the center flight feathers is visually elegant because some intact primaries are visible when the wing is folded.

Below: Cutting alternate feathers. How many is determined by trial and error. Caution: amazons which barely get off the floor indoors have been known to fly away outdoors. Air movement and a longer running start facilitate taking off.

Above: This drawing shows how the vane can be trimmed.

Below: The ring is held closed around the parrot's foot by means of a spring snap. The snap in turn is attached to the cord by means of a swivel link.

holding the bird. As previously described, the amazon is wrapped in a towel and laid on its back on a table. Then a wing is pulled out and held fast against the (soft) padding. With a short scissors having rounded points, the feathers are clipped in the manner previously described. Before the next wing is tackled, the bird is once again wrapped up firmly; care must be taken that it does not escape at this stage. With tame amazons, clipping the wings is child's play, just as the claw trimming is. One spreads a wing with one hand; with the scissors in the other, one cuts the desired feathers one by one. Care must be taken that the amazon does not bite the scissors and injure its tongue.

For an amazon, the disadvantage of clipped wings is mainly the lack of freedom of movement in emergency situations, e.g., when fleeing from others of the same species or from other pets. Once it has fluttered to the ground, the amazon cannot get up again except by climbing. Provision for this must have been made. Unflighted amazons move along the floor in a droll manner, but the danger of their catching cold on cold tiles should not be underestimated.

There have been instances where amazons began to pluck their feathers after wing clipping. This can be explained as a reaction to the loss of their wings. Feather-plucking is often an expression of frustration. Certainly clipping must be frustrating if the animal has been accustomed to flying a lot. Of course, not every clipped amazon plucks itself.

The removal of the flight-muscle tendon and the cutting of the wing by a veterinarian, as is done with decorative waterfowl, is not under discussion for amazons. Any bird which is unable to fly for the rest of its life is a pitiful creature. It cannot be foreseen whether it might not need intact wings sometime during its long life. For instance, if it should ever be put into an aviary with flighted birds, it would immediately be inferior to them. In such a case, it is an advantage if the wing feathers can grow in again.

In our opinion, if an amazon is to be taken outdoors, the best choice is to tie it by a leg. It

In the interior of Jamaica, on the River Martha Brae, Heinz Liebfarth observed both amazon species, noting that *A. agilis* occurred in pairs and *A. collaria* in small groups.

doesn't have to be done with a chain. A leash made of artificial fiber, such as is available in pet stores for cats and small dogs, is sufficient if the amazon is constantly carried on one's shoulders and is always watched. Attachment to the parrot's foot is done by means of a ring which is on the parrot chain. There are two varieties: a constantly worn ring that has an eyelet; or a ring that can be put on as needed. For tame amazons, the latter is recommended, because putting it on and taking it off is less unpleasant for the bird than a constant weight on its leg. It is important that the chain or leash have a swivelling link at the end, so that the amazon can turn as often as it wants without becoming tangled. The point is not to keep an amazon chained constantly; this method of keeping it is not suitable for these species. A leashed amazon can do very little climbing on the parrot stand and suffers from the restricted area of movement. Thus we recommend a parrot chain only for excursions outdoors with the keeper.

Facing page: Blue-fronted Amazon (*A. aestiva*).

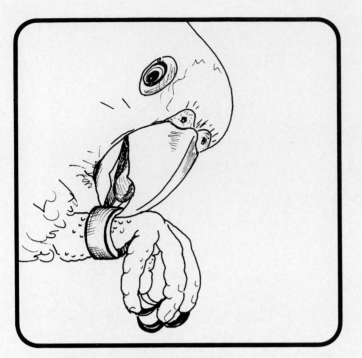

Above: Too-tight bands can irritate the foot.

Below: Heavy metal bands can be opened by hand-vises.

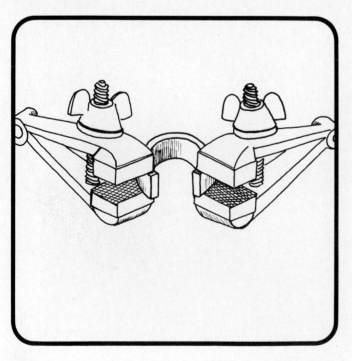

Removing Too-tight Bands A different kind of ring from the previously mentioned one is the official leg band. It is possible for it to be too tight and to cause the animal considerable pain. From constant picking with the beak, the skin on the leg becomes even more irritated, and finally the band stays fast in the swollen tissue. At this point, if it can be removed by a veterinarian without having to amputate the leg, one can consider oneself lucky. Some prevention is better. As already mentioned, the bands are required for dealers and breeders, and even for private persons, if one wants to take the amazon abroad. The band serves to identify the bird; otherwise, it may be removed. However, it should be kept as a form of documentation.

The amazon is wrapped up as described and the banded leg extended. A helper holds the animal. One needs only two combination pliers and a lot of strength. If the ring still has a few millimeters play around the leg, it is even easier. The ring is turned with the openable seam toward the observer, and the ends are bent apart just far enough to let the leg pass. Frequently the pliers will slip off because one cannot push and pull at the same time. One must take care not to injure the bird's skin when slipping the band off. It is a lot easier with two hand-vises which are fastened at exactly the same places as the pliers and then screwed tight. They cannot possibly slip off, and one can put one's whole strength into bending open the band. However, one must always be careful not to break the amazon's leg bone or to abrade the skin. Sometimes, with grown-in bands, it will be impossible to avoid a slight injury, but, fortunately, skin damage in birds heals quickly.

Tame Amazons

It is a matter for discussion among animal lovers whether amazons and other parrots should be tamed at all. Usually, together with their wildness, completely tame animals also lose the capacity to form a pair bond. After reaching sexual maturity, they cannot fully express innate behavior patterns. Once bonded to a human, they refuse to engage in contact with others of their species. However, there are exceptions.

At present, the majority of bird lovers keep amazons as single birds which are expected to say words and whole sentences after a short time, to imitate sounds and animal voices, to whistle short melodies and, besides all this, to become very affectionate. They should let their feathers be scratched and always be pleasant and lively when anybody pays attention to them. In short, as we humans see it, an amazon should give much pleasure and joy with its clownish behavior. Unfortunately, this prospect is not always realized. Many bird keepers know too little about the requirements and the behavioral disposition of their parrots. The result of improper treatment is a spoiled parrot and a disappointed owner. This need not be. If the importation of amazons, which takes place at great expense, can be justified at all, it is only by vivacious, healthy, chattering birds that feel more or less at home in the human household, even though this has nothing in common with their native habitat.

Whether an amazon is tamed or whether a pair is kept should depend on the rarity of the species. It would be too bad, for instance, if a Festive Amazon (*Amazona festiva*) were tamed as a single animal. Infrequently imported species which are not covered by the Washington Convention [CITES] but are nevertheless rare, should be permitted to breed. The numerously imported amazons can more readily be kept as single birds; who knows, however, how much longer they will be numerous?

Young amazons are the quickest to become tame. Contact with humans exclusively results in their considering the human as a mate. This event, called *imprinting* in behavioral science, takes place during a sensitive period in the life of the young birds. If taken from the nest and raised by hand, these amazons exhibit no instinct to flee from humans, but behave aggressively or fearfully towards members of their own species. At first, imprinting applies to humans in general; later, it will be noticed that a certain person is clearly preferred. This imprinting to a human is, strictly speaking, a *mis*imprinting, because it prevents the amazon from bonding with a member of its own species. It sees its keeper as a substitute partner. It does not matter which sex the animal or the keeper belong to. The rule that a male bird prefers a female keeper, and vice-versa, has since been disproved. An amazon hen can certainly accept the lady of the house as her favorite person. If she should change owners later on, she will again prefer a female keeper. Such animals are called "ladies' birds." Of course, their counterparts, "gentlemen's birds," also exist. But, as mentioned, this has nothing to do with the sex of the animal. On the other hand, if the young birds have contact only with others like themselves, they become imprinted on their own species. They will not permit a later owner to touch their bodies, let alone to scratch them. However, they can become accustomed to climbing onto the hand and to being carried around on the human's shoulder.

The mirror test is interesting in this connection: if an amazon which is imprinted on humans is faced with a mirror, it does not react particularly. But an amazon imprinted on its species will greet its mirror image with all kinds of impressive behavior, such as lowering its wings, narrowing its pupils, fluffing up the plumage on its head and neck, and spreading

Blue-fronted Amazon (*A. aestiva xanthopteryx*).

Yellow-crowned Amazon (*A. ochrocephala*).

its tail. One should be aware of the responsibility one assumes by imprinting an amazon on oneself. It is almost impossible to get a mate for the tamed animal at a later time. With each step of the taming methods described below, a part of the amazon's natural behavior is taken away.

Taming: *1. ACCLIMATION* Newly imported amazons are particularly sensitive to cold. They are best kept at room temperature. If they are hand-raised youngsters, so-called baby amazons, they must be fed some gruel-like nourishment in addition to sunflower seeds: boiled cornmeal, moistened zwieback, or baby foods, for instance (see the section on feeding). This acclimation usually takes place at the importer's, the stage between the airport and the animal dealer. Once the amazon has found a buyer, adaptation takes place to its final surroundings: life among people. Gradually it has become separated from the others of its kind. It sees more people and fewer amazons around it, until it finally has only one species left as a mate: the human. No doubt this is a difficult change. But the amazon will accept the substitute human mate and will become close to him, if it is not too disappointed in him.

Immediately after the purchase two conflicting interests meet: the amazon wants and needs peace to become accustomed to the change in place and cage, while the bird keeper is particularly interested just now in his new acquisition. He would like "to do something" with the animal immediately. However, if at all possible, he should forego this, at least on the day of the purchase itself. If the amazon can be left in its cage for the following few days, one will be least likely to spoil anything. A chase through the whole house after a bird which is capable of flight, that should return to its cage but doesn't want to, is not likely to build a relationship of trust between the animal and the human. It also is an unpleasant memory to think of the first time a clipped bird discovered the uselessness of its wings when it started from its cage, frightened by the strange surroundings. Apart from the mental shock, the bird also suffers physical pain as it crashes to the ground.

Therefore, the amazon should stay in its cage at first. In time, it will consider this space as its own and will defend it against intrusion, such as by the human hand. For this reason, tidbits should be put into the appropriate dishes, not held right in front of the beak through the opened cage door. Each time, on approaching the cage, one should bring a little something for the amazon: a cherry, a piece of a twig, or a peanut, to mention only a few. All the while, one talks to it, calls it by name, and then turns away, even if the amazon, still distrustful, will not yet eat its tidbit. Sometime during the next fifteen minutes it will test the offered item with its beak, perhaps when it feels unobserved. Gradually, the amazon will learn to appreciate the human hand as the bringer of food and will make a connection between it and the human voice. It learns that the various people in the family will not harm it and that the cage is its own territory. It announces this by the sounds it now begins to make. In strange territory, the bird will not sing or whistle; it tries to be as unobtrusive as possible. But where it feels at home, it is not at all reticent.

One should wait until the amazon demonstrates this sense of security by uttering these sounds, before letting it out of its cage. It goes without saying that the position of the cage should not be changed, particularly during the period of acclimation, so that the amazon may always observe the room from the same point of view, which enables it to find its way back to its cage after its first excursions. When doing cleaning around and in the cage during the acclimation period, care must be taken to avoid quick movements, which the animal might misinterpret as threats. It is immensely important that the hands of the human not be associated with negative experiences, since the amazon is supposed to become hand-tame.

2. HAND-TAMING To meet the expectations of many keepers, an amazon must exhibit the characteristics of a well-trained household pet: it must not bite; it should not be afraid of people; it should readily allow itself to be taken from its cage and put back in. All of this is far from natural in a wild animal, and the amazon was just taken from the primeval forest; it is not a domesticated pet like a dog or a cat. The road to having a tame parrot is, therefore, not always easy. Even someone who acquires a super-tame amazon chick has no guarantee that it will always remain that way. As it grows older, it becomes more aggressive. Every amazon is different, and there are no commonly valid rules for taming. What was successful with your neighbor's "Coco" may be completely wrong for "Lora." Therefore, one must first sensitively discover which taming strategy is most effective with one's own parrot.

An amazon can first be accustomed to a wooden stick, on which it has to climb. Gradually the stick is shortened, and eventually —with luck—the bird will perch on the hand. This method runs into difficulties with amazons capable of flying: after the bird takes off from a perch which is held in the hand, the stick may jerk upward and hit the bird in the abdomen. This jerking effect is the most serious with a broomstick and an amazon the size of a Blue-fronted Amazon (*Amazona aestiva*) or larger. Many amazons will become frightened forever of hand-held perches. Moreover, it is not certain that the amazon will later recognize the presented hand as a possible perch, once it has been trained to climb onto a stick.

An innate behavior trait of the amazon facilitates taming to the hand: the threatening gesture with the foot. Wild amazons turn their foot toward their attacker, with toes open and needle-sharp claws. To the attacking animal this signals a readiness for defense. As a rule, the foot is raised in situations where the amazon does not want, or is unable, to leave its perch. Many parrot owners think that this gesture means that the bird wants to "shake hands." Of course, this is a mistaken interpretation. If a finger is presented, the bird will grab it with its foot. It is possible that it won't bite; courageous animals will, though. This is no reason to suddenly draw back and frighten the bird. In later attempts, the bird

will be able to get on without biting, once the amazon has learned that the finger will not press it further.

The next step involves getting the amazon to step up. This can be accomplished by moving the finger in the direction of the animal's abdomen. It will automatically climb up, since it does not want to fall over backwards. However, timid amazons will retreat so far into the cage that they hang upside down. In such cases, the time is not ripe to try this method. Other amazons are "backward steppers": the hand has to be held in back of their toes; they then step backwards. Others will first test each perch with the beak. This must not be misunderstood as biting. It is often only a touching with the upper mandible. If the hand is withdrawn when this occurs, the bird will never climb up. It is also important to know that parrots tend to climb upward on inclined branches. This satisfies their need for security, which a bird, of course, is more likely to seek higher up rather than below. Even on the human arm the amazon will try to move higher. For this reason, the arm must be extended so that it does not go down toward the elbow, but forms a continuous incline. Once the amazon has gotten to the shoulder, it will be reluctant to leave this vantage point. The bird will defend this spot against any approaching hand. Apparently it likes to sit on the same level as the keeper's head. If one wants the amazon to leave the shoulder, one extends his arm obliquely upward. The bird will then climb in the direction of the hand, since this is even higher. If this doesn't work, one can crouch in front of the cage and let the bird climb up. Flighted amazons can sometimes be dislodged by a strong shrug, but most amazons have had their wings clipped and must depend on climbing. This situation makes taming easier: as a result of the constant contact, the amazon becomes more quickly accustomed to its keeper's hand or shoulder than if it were just to fly away. Only very confident animals will climb downward. One can see this even from their behavior in the cage: some will pick up pieces of fruit that have

Breeding pair of Yellow-crowned Amazons (*A. ochrocephala ochrocephala***) allowed freedom in the kitchen.**

Red-lored Amazon (*A. autumnalis diadema*).

fallen to the floor; others will leave them there untouched. Once an amazon has been tamed to the extent that it can be carried around the house, much has been achieved.

3. FURTHER CONTACT As the next stage of taming, there is foot scratching. It can be developed from "shaking hands." The toes are carefully petted, especially on the underside. The amazon enjoys this, particularly because the old horny scales are rubbed off. Once the bird keeper is allowed to massage the toes of the animal, he will also be able to trim the claws with less difficulty. The bird is used to the situation and is not frightened by it.

By the time an amazon has been owned for several months, many new feather sheaths have begun to sprout. Those on the neck and the head cannot be preened by the bird itself; at best, they can only be partially groomed with the foot. In the wild, these areas are preened by conspecifics; this is known as allopreening. A singly kept bird is dependent on the help of the human. To have new feathers unsheathed is an urgent need. Nevertheless, the amazon will decide when it wants to have its head scratched. Premature attempts are parried with a swipe of the beak. One must wait until the amazon

The foot is covered with scales.

exhibits the following behavior: ruffling the crown and neck feathers, holding the head at an angle, or scratching the head feathers with its foot. But even now, not every touch is welcome. One has to discover the proper spots: around the cheeks, the eyes, the ears, the neck, the forehead, or the cere. After a while one can try to touch other parts of the plumage. The amazon will quickly indicate whether this is welcome. In any case, few parrots let their backs be petted; to try to start there would be wrong.

It is soon established who in the family has the right to do this or that to the bird and who does not. The latter is lower in rank, so to speak, than the amazon. This is the equivalent of the social structure of the flock in the wilderness. A lot depends on the relationship of the human flock member to the amazon. Whoever is timid will be most likely to get a swipe of the beak; henceforth he has to make way for the amazon and will not be readily allowed to remove it from its perch and hold it in his hand.

When interacting with amazons, one tends to use a human yardstick to judge its behavior (see the Introduction to this book). But it would not be correct to state that an amazon is cunning, jealous, mean, or that it laughs maliciously. Concepts of good and evil are foreign to it; it knows only the rules of the battle for survival in its environment. Thus far there has been one point common to our training methods: the bird must be able to trust its keeper. It adopts the desired behavior of its own free will.

The opposite, forced taming, is an abuse of the animal and leads to a mentally injured bird that will certainly not give any pleasure. A hundred years ago, forcible methods were still widespread. Once daily the amazon was grabbed with hands wearing thick, special gloves, set into the lap of the keeper, and forced to remain still. This continued until the bird gave up resisting. Russ wrote that parrots should be forced into the smallest possible cages during "training," and that one should talk down to them from above, against the light, to let them feel the power of the human. Even Russ warned against punishing the birds by striking them, since they feel the blows not as punishment, but as an attack, and will not show the desired change in their behavior. If an amazon is already fully grown when it comes into human hands, taming it will require a long time; in some cases, it will not be successful. The best solution is to keep such birds in pairs in a roomy aviary, even if the pair do not go on to breed.

Talking: *1. BASICS* Imitating human speech is directly connected with imprinting. Acoustical stimuli absorbed during this sensitive phase are learned and can later be reproduced. In parrots this learning period is not precisely fixed in time, so that even with increasing age learning can take place, though not as intensively as during youth. In other birds, the period of sensitivity ends abruptly at a certain age, and what has not been learned by then can never be picked up.

In birds, sound is formed at the lower end of the trachea by the syrinx and its membranes. The elastic air sac which surrounds the syrinx tightens the membranes and causes them to vibrate. The upper throat (larynx) and the space formed by the beak and mouth act as additional resonators. (Hachfeld, *Die Voliere*, 1981/2). As a rule, birds will articulate only sounds which derive from their innate, instinctual endowment. These utterances occur involuntarily, i.e. without the intention of imparting this or that information to the others of the species. The hearers react to certain stimuli by means of innate behavior, not by evaluating the messages rationally, the way we humans do. Calls and songs are partly innate, partly learned from parent animals.

Parrots and parakeets, crows and mockingbirds will utter not only those sounds which are innate or learned from others of their species, but also melodies foreign to them. The reason why has not yet been uncovered completely. In mockingbirds, it is suspected that a wider spectrum of sounds ensures a better chance of finding a mate; this was determined during research on mockingbirds (Hachfeld). Schmidt explains the phenomenon as follows in his mynah book: "Their own acoustical possibilities of expression do not appear sufficient to express the inner tensions connected with courtship, making threats, reproduction of the vocal signals from their own period of growth, warnings, and other socially related communication. "It is striking that parrots (and mynahs) with their vocal tools can imitate human speech, among others things, perfectly. This skill was developed in the course of evolution, long before their first contact with humans; what purpose it serves is controversial.

Konrad Lorenz wrote (in his book *Er redete mit dem Vieh, den Vögeln und den Fischen*) that parrots can never learn to use their speech to attain even a simple goal. The talent therefore is useless. Otto zur Strassen refuted this in his essay ("Zweckdienliches Sprechen beim Graupapagei") on purposeful speech in the Grey Parrot. He holds the opinion that there must exist among parrots a highly developed acoustical system of communication, which includes purposeful speech. Its utility for the survival of the species must have a value within the species, either in the life of the pair or in the community of the flock. Schmidt sees the principal purpose in the fact that parrots are not limited to their innate repertoire of vocal utterances only, but are open to learning to the extent that they can use imitation for the intelligent improvement of their living conditions and the organization of their lives and their social relations. This the amazon indeed does, even in captivity. Talking results from the inclination of the amazon to engage in a social relationship with its companion, adopting his vocal utterances. The keeper assumes the role of the mate if he devotes enough time to the animal. However, imitation is not limited to the speech of the keeper; it extends to all other acoustic stimuli which are consciously perceived by the parrot.

2. TALKING INSTRUCTION Instruction in talking is most successful when the teacher utilizes the sensitive period of the young animal. One does best to begin on the day after purchase. At first the amazon is addressed only

Above: Tail feathers of a Yellow-crowned Amazon (*A. ochrocephala ochrocephala*). All are the fourth lateral feather from the outside, from successive molts at one, two, and three years of age. It is easy to see how the coloration changes.

Left, above: Double Yellow-headed Amazon (*A. ochrocephala oratrix*).

Left, below: Orange-winged Amazon (*A. amazonica*). Amazons enjoy being scratched, especially in those areas not accessible by the beak.

Facing page: Double Yellow-head (*A. ochrocephala oratrix*), about 16 months old.

with a simple word. This can be its name, or *hello, come here,* or similar words. After about three weeks, it will make the first vocalization, or a babbling series of syllables, in which one can hear something, with the help of a little imagination. By this time, it will fly to the keeper of its own volition or will at least be interested in him. With radio music on, the amazon is very likely to sing. After four weeks, it will holler loudly along with the vacuum cleaner. It has adapted to the extent that it grooms itself uninhibitedly, undertakes explorations in and on the cage, and begins to molt its tail feathers. After six weeks, a strong growth of feathers can be noticed. The amazon will allow itself to be scratched, but may bite if one tries to put it back into its cage. After seven to eight weeks, one can detect for the first time correct imitation of a word. Success in teaching will come more quickly if one goes along with the playful sounds of the amazon. A tip: let the amazon name itself—try to hear a name in its chattering. Repeat this often (slowly and with emphasis), so that the bird will learn to pronounce it clearly.

This first bit of success will affect further developments. An example may illustrate this. Let us assume that you wish to call your amazon "Donald." For hours you repeat this one word. During its evening vocalizing the amazon says anything but *Donald.* It prefers successions of syllables like *gurre, urrig, rigo, rido, rida.* So you must change your approach. Give up on *Donald* for the time being; pick a word or a name which you hear in those syllables, such as *Frieda* or *Fridolin.* The amazon will repeat this within a short time. The word *Donald* can be taught later. The amazon will now call its keeper with this first word, learned because it discovers that this is rewarded with attention, i.e., positively reinforced. Most words in the vocabulary of an amazon are learned not through intensive teaching, but through frequently repeated situational speaking: "Good morning!—Hello!—Goodbye!—Quiet!—Go to your cage!—What are you doing?" Many amazons (and Grey Parrots) say *Jako* even if they have been given another

name. The reason, in the opinion of the authors, is the fact that a parrot is often addressed with "*Ja, komm!*" ("Come on!") which it will slurringly repeat as "Jako". Thus, the name Coco may have been formed from "Come, come."

If eliciting particular expressions is the goal, the task is much more difficult. If one wants speech instruction to be successful, one must use those times of the day when the parrot is relaxed and has an open ear for its keeper. This mostly happens in the evening. A narrowing of the pupils serves as an indication that the animal is listening attentively. There has to be at least eye contact between keeper and bird, and physical contact is even better. Naturally, the amazon must not be distracted by other things while one is saying something that is to be learned.

Amazons like to whistle, or, more correctly, they like to imitate human whistling. It is in the keeper's interest to proceed with caution here. Certainly each bird keeper is proud when his charge has learned to "flute" a melody correctly. But who will enjoy the loud, shrill whistling that one has carelessly demonstrated to the parrot? In the long run, this can drive you up the wall. But the amazon is innocent. There is no point in trying to break it of this habit; therefore, it is probably better not to show it how to whistle piercingly in the first place. In any case, one has to consider that the capacity for learning speech will be diminished if its memory is filled with various whistles.

3. IMITATIVE BEHAVIOR Otto zur Strassen distinguishes the following five steps:

1. Mere imitation (exact reproduction, but meaningless chattering)
2. Association (situation and sound are associated; situation is the trigger for the sound)
3. Abstraction (formation of a concept, e.g., a gurgling sound for all liquids, the name of a child for all children)
4. Anticipation (uttering of a sound in advance of the expected situation, e.g., *goodbye,*

before anyone leaves)

5. Purposeful speech (uttering of a sound in advance of a desired situation, e.g., *goodbye*, if the parrot wants to be left alone, and the person should leave the room).

Schmidt establishes the following classification:

1. Simple imitation of sounds (mechanical imitation of any sounds)
2. Transposition and variation (varying melodies, interchanging syllables, creation of new words)
3. Utterances related to the situation (*good morning*, when the cage is uncovered)
4. Purposeful speech for the fulfillment of a need (*come in*, said by a bird which has been left alone)
5. Anticipation of expected and/or desired events through suitable utterances (imitation of the sound of a popping cork upon seeing a bottle).

Both authors document their statements with a wealth of examples which are sometimes astonishing. But one thing is certain: the parrots do not understand the meaning of the words they are saying. If they answer questions correctly, it is not because of understanding, but because their amazing memory supplies the correct answer at the required moment. And this happens only because the answer is rewarded, be it with laughter or increased attention on the part of the audience. Besides, the brain capacity of parrots is not sufficient to learn syntax or grammatical sentence construction as chimpanzees can, for instance. These anthropoid apes are (within certain limits) capable of language. Unfortunately, they cannot articulate with the vocal tools they possess and are, therefore, not able to speak. With parrots, the reverse is the case.

Day-to-day Care: *1. BASICS* The amazon's natural need for gnawing and movement and its desire for social contact must be met, if it is not to adopt a substitute behavior, such as screeching and feather plucking. It should constantly be offered new twigs, small branches, pieces of wood (e.g., scraps from a carpentry shop), pine cones, and similar material for gnawing. Besides this, there is the varied diet. Hanging a small box with a hole in the front in the cage provides an interesting object for a sexually mature amazon, because it is similar to a breeding cavity. The amazon will spend hours working on the entrance, which gets more and more enlarged. In the end, the cardboard is completely chewed, and the box has to be replaced by a new one.

The amazon should be given the opportunity to become accustomed to several places in the house that are its own. This territory can include the cage, climbing tree, parrot stand, backs of various chairs, windowsill, window handle, perches on the wall, and many others. Its perching places depend on the flying abilities of the amazon. Perching on open doors is undesirable, but probably not completely avoidable. For one thing, this is a source of considerable danger. How easily could toes be pinched! Also, sitting on top of the door leads to its getting soiled. In this connection, a small board to catch the droppings can be mounted 30 cm. below the upper edge of the door. This is easier to clean than the entire door and the floor. However, it is best right from the start to keep the amazon from flying even a single time to the top of a door. The door to its room should always remain closed. To the right and left of the door, other perches should be provided; then it will not select the door as a landing place. If it has had the opportunity to get acquainted with this ideally high perch several times, it will hardly be possible to break the habit. Many amazons will even fly onto closed doors and hook their claws to the door frame.

2. DROPPINGS Bird droppings in the house are a real problem for many housewives, and yet it can be surmounted quite easily. By the way, the droppings are firm in consistency, semimoist, green-white in color, and covered with a mucous sac which barely adheres to fabrics. To predict when the amazon is going to drop its next little pile, one has to study its

Above: Yellow-crowned Amazon (*A. ochrocephala*).

Below: Mealy Amazon (*A. farinosa*).

behavior exactly. Birds have very quick digestion in order to carry as little ballast as possible when they fly. If one gives the amazon a piece of fruit, the corresponding droppings will be excreted after about half an hour. One can almost wait for it. Apart from such between-meal treats, the consistency of which is mirrored by the droppings, amazons frequently feel the urge to evacuate. This often happens in typical situations; the most important ones are listed here: For instance, a bird prefers to "drop ballast" before taking off. Consequently, if the amazon is not taken by hand from the cage but is allowed to fly toward the keeper, it has a suitable opportunity to take care of this need before one plays with it. If the amazon sits on the keeper's shoulder for a longish period of time, defecation must be expected. If the bird becomes restless and climbs back and forth without motivation, it should be put on its stand. Often, the change of position alone suffices as a "dropping impulse." The event must be remarked upon by the keeper with a rewarding word. In this manner, the amazon learns to use its stand as the preferred place for excretion. However, it will not become completely housebroken. In many instances it does its business wherever it happens to be at the time. It sits with legs spread wide, pushes its rear down, and lifts the tail—feathers somewhat. If one notices this position, the bird can quickly be set aside. It will take care of the evacuation, after getting over its surprise, on its stand.

If one keeps his eye on the amazon, he can anticipate every excretion and by fast action can prevent clothing, upholstered furniture, and carpeting from being soiled. Only when sitting on one's own shoulder is the animal not in the field of vision. An amazon will also empty its intestine *after* physical exercise. For instance, after it has been sitting quietly for two hours in its cage and is then taken out to "waddle" a few steps on the floor, it will certainly pause in its walk to defecate, and will continue its walk afterwards. Constant walking back and forth in the cage to attract attention is also a physical exercise which causes evacuation. Finally, psychic stress (fear, fright) will lead to a quick

Yellow-naped Amazon (*A. ochrocephala auropalliata*) becoming accustomed to stepping onto a stick.

evacuation of droppings. If a salesperson in the pet shop takes an amazon from its cage to show it, this has to be expected. The same holds true when one attempts to catch an untamed animal in the house. "Fear-droppings" are mostly smaller or thinner in consistency than normal.

The subject of droppings has been treated at such length because it shows how closely an amazon can and should be observed. This duty of the parrot keeper is very important. Knowledge of the animal's behavior facilitates contact with it, as well as progress in taming and speech lessons. Even if the amazon cannot fulfill the expectation of mimicry set for it, it is an interesting creature, well worth being studied.

3. DANGERS By instinct the amazon is equipped only for life in the wild, not for life in a human household. While there is no danger of being captured by a predator, there are other life-threatening situations from which it has to be protected. The possibility of getting its feet pinched in doors has already been mentioned. Climbing into cupboards and drawers (attractive areas for cavity breeders) entails the danger of suffocation if the doors or drawers are suddenly closed. There must be no electrical cords or outlets near the cage, climbing tree, and so forth, because these are easily chewed apart by the amazon. It may ignore the cord for months, until one day it begins to "work" on it after all. Amazons with clipped wings often move along the floor, and here too they sometimes can get to electrical cords. These should be removed or made inaccessible. A hot burner on the stove, a pot with boiling water, and a package containing medicine represent other sources of danger. The parrot must not be permitted to tear apart cigarettes. Smoking in the same room is also unhealthy; an amazon should not be forced to become a passive smoker throughout its life.

If an amazon flies into a window pane, it may suffer a concussion, or worse, depending on its speed upon impact. Large cockatoos have flown through closed(!) windows to freedom, but nothing similar is reported about amazons. Yet with thin, single-glazed windows, this might be possible. The amazon can be accustomed to window panes (if draperies are not used) by occasionally putting the cage next to the window in question. From the cage, the beak can acquire familiarity with the strange material, glass. Impact from a short distance is not very dangerous. The amazon will soon learn to respect the pane as an invisible wall. Silhouettes of predators made from black cardboard and glued to the pane have not always proven successful. As a rule, amazons escape through open windows; one left slightly ajar may already be open wide enough to permit the bird passage. The bird keeper must develop the habit of never leaving open any windows in the territory of the amazon. If an amazon nevertheless gets into a room with open windows, it is important to remain calm. Normally it will not fly through the window, but will head for a familiar landing place.

An amazon will often fly after its keeper when he leaves the room. If he should go — by mistake — onto the balcony, it can be expected that the flighted bird will follow, wanting only to get onto his shoulder. It should be permitted to land there, and the keeper should go back into the room. On the other hand, if one jerks with fright, tries to grab the bird, and shouts, the amazon will fly off to seek open spaces.

Many dangers await the parrot outdoors: cold, lack of food, cats, predatory birds, rain, and infections are mentioned only in passing. Even in the house, cats and dogs can be dangerous to the amazon. In principle, it can defend itself with claws and beak, can fly away (if its wings are not clipped), or can frighten off four-legged creatures with ear-piercing shrieks; but whether these defense mechanisms will work is not certain. Cats and dogs are not all equally dangerous. Those that chase after birds in the yard may also have designs on green hookbills. However, the authors have observed how two "dangerous" cats exhibited absolute disinterest in an amazon that talked very well. The talking confused them. A dog should be accustomed at an early age to an amazon already living in the household and should be brought up to leave the bird in peace.

However, if one keeps other pets besides, one does not do justice to the amazon. The bird requires the total attention of its keeper, not merely a part of it.

"Bad Habits" Actually, the concept of bad habits should be applied only in regard to improper behavior traits of humans, not in connection with amazons. Bad habits of the keeper are, for instance, giving kisses, taking the parrot along to bed, or teasing it with a finger. Leaving a bird alone for hours or keeping it exclusively in a cage are also incorrect for the care of these species.

What is seen as unacceptable activity in the *amazon* (destructiveness, for instance) is only a consequence of improper care. Just as lifelong incarceration in a small parrot cage is detrimental, so is the opposite, total freedom in the house. An amazon would not be normal if it were to leave the many details of interior decoration alone, uninvestigated. Designed by nature to undertake mile-long excursions through tropical rain forests, it finds in a house a smaller but even more varied field of activity for its beak. Houseplants are destroyed, tables cleared, and wallpaper pulled from the wall. A pencil is turned into splinters within five minutes; a ball-point pen takes a little longer. For the bird keeper, this is a nuisance; for the amazon it is sometimes a mortal danger. But the bird will never learn that it is not allowed to do these things. The conclusions for the bird keeper are: (1) The amazon in free flight must be supervised constantly. (2) It must be offered suitable gnawing material outside of its cage. (3) It must be kept away from unsuitable gnawing material. This last can be effected by installing fear-inspiring objects. Many amazons are afraid of gloves, others of stuffed animals or dolls. These things can be placed in front of desk lamps, on upholstered furniture, or next to flowerpots. Where scare tactics are not possible, removal—with amicable consequences—of the amazon from the forbidden area helps. More often by far it happens that an amazon is not given sufficient free space; this leads us to the three well-known bad habits: screeching, biting, and plucking.

1. SCREECHING First, on the topic of screeching: How much an amazon screeches or whether it does it at all depends primarily on its temperament. In general, it can be said only that certain situations and circumstances especially tend to encourage screeching. For instance, an amazon screeches as a reaction to other loud noises, such as vacuum cleaners, all kinds of motors, radio, TV, musical instruments, dogs, or loud conversation. By screeching, it intends to impress the other sources of noise. Second, screeching can be an expression of *joie de vivre* and well-being. The amazon will screech without provocation, mostly once in the morning and in the evening. In the wild, territorial claims are thus announced. Third, the amazon screeches from dissatisfaction and boredom; for instance, when it has nothing to nibble on, would like to get out of its cage, or seeks contact with its keeper. Several reasons can work together, and an amazon that has reason to screech often, can come to do it all the time.

A responsible keeper will take precautions to keep the screeching in bounds, if it cannot be suppressed completely. To counter screeching from boredom, it helps to offer new gnawing material constantly. A parrot stand is also useful, since it widens the territory of the bird. Amazons not capable of flight can be carried from the cage to the stand, or vice-versa, when they screech. The stand can also be located in another room, namely the one in which the keeper happens to be at the time. When the amazon has company, it will not screech. Screeching in response to vacuuming is the first screeching the parrot keeper gets to know. Indeed, parrot keeping and vacuuming are closely linked. The amazon will outdo the loud noise, but stops as soon as the motor has become silent. If, while vacuuming, one picks up the amazon and talks calmly to it, it will listen to the human voice, sense itself to be important, and in many instances will refrain from further screeching.

The following measures may help to control

Above: Festive Amazon (*A. festiva*).

Below: This is neither a Blue-fronted nor a "Yellow-cheeked" Amazon, but an Orange-winged Amazon (*A. amazonica*).

screeching in the morning and evening: Dawn and twilight are bypassed by the use of shutters or shades, which cause a sudden darkening or illumination of the room. At night, however, artificial light must remain on until the amazon has eaten. The light should be turned off around 8 PM. Complete darkness prevents all screeching, but it does not conform to natural conditions. The amazon needs a certain degree of light at night in order to orient itself. For this reason, one should refrain from darkening of the room completely, or at least to delay it until the animal has settled down.

Screeching from boredom is often a learned behavior, since it always results in the keeper's paying attention to the animal. This is exactly the outcome it wanted to obtain. In effect, the bird keeper has "rewarded" the screeching. It is better to reward words spoken by the amazon, such as *hello* or *come here*. It will always use these expressions when it wants company. They should be responded to as quickly as possible, before the bird switches to screeching. On the other hand, there are amazons that will continue to screech despite the presence and coaxing of the keeper. This phenomenon can be compared to feather eating or plucking. It is a manifestation of a captivity neurosis, which is especially seen in older wild-caught birds. They screech for hours for a mate. Whether they really will get along with another amazon is uncertain. If it is impossible to get them to pair, the screeching will not lessen; the two will screech together, though for different reasons.

2. BITING Young, very tame amazons that have been raised by humans do not bite at all. They touch the finger with their pointed beaks very carefully, without inflicting even the slightest pain. With increasing age, this changes. They learn to use their beaks to further their interests. The initially weak beaks nip more strongly for a time before, suddenly, they really grab. There are two courses the bird keeper can choose: One may let oneself be bitten several times without letting the amazon know that this is painful. This way, the amazon learns that biting is useless. If one screams or

Yellow-crowned Amazon (*A. ochrocephala ochrocephala*). The male, 10 years old, shows more yellow than the female, 3 years old.

pulls back the hand, the act of biting would be positively reinforced. Tape can be put on thumb and index finger beforehand; these won't bother the bird as much as gloves will. This course is not for everyone, nor does it always have the desired outcome. Some amazons come to consider fingers something that can be chewed on at will. The alternative is this: to screech like the amazon ("*Aehh!*") at the slightest use of pressure with the beak. One can observe this behavior among a group of amazons in an aviary. The amazon learns that the finger is very delicate and will treat it with adequate consideration. This method is especially effective for the keeper, on whom the amazon is imprinted, but less so for strangers. One should never present a finger to an amazon and then pull it back quickly when the beak responds. Animals that are constantly confined to a cage and cannot adequately defend themselves especially suffer from this "game." Of course, sometimes when a finger is proffered with good intentions, it is bitten. This is the reason why bloody fingers are no rarity in bird parks.

The longer one has contact with an amazon, the less one has to fear its beak. Biting is usually a defensive reaction, as, for instance, when the amazon feels cornered or cannot avoid physical contact. In the course of time both the keeper and the amazon will learn to judge correctly the opponent's actions. A slight opening of the beak, for instance, may indicate in advance that the amazon does not want to be touched at the moment. This must be respected. Conversely, the amazon learns that the outstretched hand does not threaten anything untoward, but that it is merely an invitation for the bird to sit on it. In turn, the keeper knows that the amazon does not bite if it holds onto his fingers with its beak while climbing on, for example. Amazons that have experienced much unpleasantness in the course of their life in captivity are constantly on the defensive and bite equally frequently. Here, restraint has to be exercised for years, until the amazon has learned to be trusting.

3. PLUCKING   One distinguishes between feather eating and feather plucking, depending on whether the feathers are bitten off or pulled out. According to recent interpretations, both are predominantly psychological disturbances. Thus far the causes have not been determined exactly, but the following are suspected: boredom, lack of novelty, having nothing to do, loss or absence of a mate (human or amazon), loss of accustomed surroundings, and having its wings clipped. Plucking or feather eating is a protest of the bird against the unbearable position in which it finds itself. Often, an organism will react to such situations with illness, because its defenses against infections are diminished. In the case of the feather-damaging parrot, there is no illness. An inner compulsion forces the animal to mutilate and inflict pain on itself. In such cases, only a change in living conditions can bring about an improvement. One has to devote more time to the bird, perhaps taking it along to work, or, with animals imprinted on their own species, moving the bird from its cage to an aviary with others of its kind is in order.

Of course, other measures must be taken if the plucking is caused by itching skin. The possible causes are: too low humidity; in fewer instances, ectoparasites like mites; in other cases, a deficiency of certain nutrients enters the question.

In *Die Gefiederte Welt* (1977, p. 48 and 1978, p. 114), authors Schernekau and Schmitt state the opinion that lack of cooking salt is a possible cause of plucking. Dr. M. Heidenreich, in an essay in *Die Voliere*, 1979/2, asserts an opposing point of view. He reminds us that a salt content more than 0.8% in the food can bring about the first signs of poisoning. However, Dr. Heidenreich also considers broadening the diet to be sound therapy. Nevertheless, in all cases, one should not attack the symptoms by mechanical or chemical measures instead of eliminating the cause.

Experiences   The last paragraphs in this chapter are devoted to three experiences with tame amazons, though they have nothing to do with their talking abilities. Here the amazon should not be viewed as a funny clown that makes opportune replies, but as a child of the primeval forest that does not find it easy to make its way in our surroundings. Sometimes its instinctive behavior leads to encounters that are very exciting for both human and animal.

1. "AMAZON ESCAPED" . . . is something one can read during the summer months in many Lost ads. How this can happen is described by a bird keeper in her own words:

"My amazon flies after me through the entire house and always lands on my shoulder. When I call it, it comes immediately. It regurgitates seeds and wants to feed me. I assume that it considers me its mate. I often took it out into the yard in its cage. But eventually carrying its large cage became too cumbersome, and I bought a small cage for the stay in the yard. Since it is only a few meters from the house to the yard, I simply took the amazon out on my hand, holding its toes with my thumb. It allowed this without resisting. In the yard, I put it into the smaller cage. One day, I thought that the amazon might sit on top of the cage, especially since a perch was mounted there. And really, it did not fly away.

Nevertheless, I felt uneasy about the whole thing, and I decided in the future to put it into the garden cage again. The next day it happened: the amazon resisted being put into the cage and pulled out of my hand. A few wingbeats, and it sat on the fence. I called it, but it wouldn't come. Very slowly, I approached it, my arm extended so it could get on. It had come to me this way in the house innumerable times. But this time the bird reacted differently. It flew up and landed in a tall tree, on the lowest branch. I went back, fetched the cage, and put it under the tree. The amazon now flew three branches higher up. When I attempted to get it to climb onto a broomstick, that was the end altogether. It disappeared behind the next house. It sat on the ground in a driveway. It did not move away when I got in front of it and slowly began to crouch down. It did not appear to recognize me. It was breathing heavily. As my hand got closer, it started once again and flew straight into a hedge. I rushed there and grabbed it impulsively. It bit my hand quite badly, but I held tight. And somehow I managed to get it back into the house."

This incident is instructive in several respects. Amazons escape not only through open windows or doors, but also because their owners deliberately take them outside, believing that their special bird would never fly away. The following experiences are still more likely to cause a smile, but here too it must be emphasized that for the amazon it was a serious proposition, which should cause us to reflect.

2. THE OBJECT OF TERROR   This is about the strange behavior of an Orange-winged Amazon (*Amazona amazonica*). The animal, a male about four years old, is kept by a single lady. It is tame, lets itself be petted, and says a few words. However, when its owner has guests, the bird, usually so peaceful, becomes completely changed: full of aggression, it attacks its keeper, biting her and flying off again, which leads the surprised visitors to believe that the lady may have exaggerated a little in her description of the well-mannered bird. For a while the bird keeper had no explanation why the bird behaved so crazily when guests were present. "It is jealous," she said, without quite believing it herself. One day, when she returned from shopping and did not immediately remove her wig as usual, the bird began to attack. As soon as it was let out of the cage, it flew to its keeper's shoulder and removed the wig from her head with a well-aimed whack of its beak, sending it in a high arc over the cage and the climbing tree.

The amazon had become accustomed to its keeper's not wearing a wig. Apparently, it saw this as a foreign object on its owner's head, which had to be fought off. Since all the lady's acquaintances know her only *with* her wig, she is forced to wear it at home when she has visitors. This brings out the amazon behavior just described. It is impossible, and will remain so, for the bird keeper to show her normally tame charge to strangers without letting them in on the secret of her always attractive hairdo.

3. SCENE OF CRIME: KITCHEN   During a birthday visit, the authors had the following experience with their amazon: Mother was still busy making a Black Forest cherry cake. Meanwhile, in the living room, the amazon was let out of its cage. It flew off straightaway into the kitchen. Since it was not familiar with any

Fruit to fill the crocks is prepared while a Double Yellow-head and a Cockatiel look on.

landing places there, it circled around several times and finally landed—greatly frightening the housewife—in a bowl. With wings spread, the animal sank up to its belly into a gelatinous mass of cherries which had been prepared to fill the cake. Though the amazon was freed within seconds from its unfortunate position, some of the gooey cake filling continued to stick to it. Even the tamest amazon is reluctant to allow itself to be bathed as thoroughly as was necessary after this landing. Dry again, the feathers on the abdomen were still as stiff as freshly starched laundry, and it took two more days before they were again as soft as feathers usually are.

These are the three reports. The authors are interested in hearing of further experiences with amazons from their readers; please address them in the care of the publisher.

Facing page, above: Breeding pair of White-fronted Amazons (*A. albifrons*) in a nest box with their eggs.
Below: Blue-cheeked Amazon (*A. dufresniana rhodocorytha*): fully grown male on the left, young female on the right. The different ages cause the differences in coloration.

Breeding

Sex Determination Naturally, the sex of the animals is of interest to the breeder. In most species of amazons it is not possible to determine sex at first glance: males and females have the same coloration. One exception, for instance, is the White-fronted Amazon (*Amazona albifrons*) (see the section on this species). Other species of amazons are more difficult to tell apart. Strictly speaking, only endoscopic determination of sex can give hundred-percent certainty. In this procedure, the veterinarian inserts a lighted probe 3 mm. thick into the previously anesthetized animal to determine the presence of testes or ovaries. This procedure is well worthwhile, particularly with rare species. A word of caution: after waking from the anesthesia, some birds flutter uncontrollably around the transport cage. Therefore, the cage should have soft padding on the inside.

R. Low mentions another scientific method for sex determination which is used at the San Diego Zoo: testing the droppings or other tissue samples for the presence of estrogen or testosterone (female or male sex hormones). However, this procedure is not yet practiced here [Germany].

So far, amazons have been (and still are) recognized as belonging to a given sex by the shape of the head, by the distance between the pelvic bones, and by their behavior. The male has a larger, but flatter head that extends further back before sloping off to the neck. Despite the flatter head, the distance from the eye to the top of the head is greater. The beak is more massive and wider. The shape of the female's head is rounder. In the back, the head is more shallowly sloped. The distance from the top of the head to the eye is smaller. The beak is narrower. With only one animal, these characteristics cannot always be discerned adequately. The size of the body in particular depends upon age and the species. Only when several amazons can be compared with one another can reasonably sure conclusions about sex be made. The distance between the pelvic bones offers another possibility for making a determination, and not only in amazons. In the female animal, the pelvic bones are farther apart because eggs have to pass through. However, young females may still have closely spaced pelvic bones. These bones can be felt with the finger in the area of the vent. A wide distance is one in which the index finger will fit between the bone ends.

Observation of their behavior also allows conclusions about the sex of the animals. Although courting behavior itself, voice, and an interest in nesting cavities are not characteristic of either sex, other criteria have been discovered:

- Males more than females sit upright on their perches. Sometimes, females flatten themselves, ducklike.
- Because of the position of the hip bones, females sit with legs farther apart than males, which keep their feet closer together.
- Females are more likely to bite, but males tend to be louder.
- Females are more likely to go onto the floor of the cage.
- Males spread their tail feathers more frequently; females usually hold their tail feathers closed.

If the animals are allowed to choose their own mates (if a group of amazons is kept, that is), in theory, one gets breeding pairs without determining sex. But even so, that breeding will follow is still not guaranteed: sometimes two cocks or two hens get along with each other very well, and the keeper may even notice copulatory activity—but there will be no breeding!

Pairing for Breeding Someone who has selected an amazon cock and a hen according to the methods described in the previous chapter is now the owner of a *pair*, but not necessarily of a *breeding pair*. If the two birds do not get along, there will be fights over food and perches, which not only look dangerous, but really are. In captivity, the space amazons have at their disposal is always limited. In contrast to the situation in the wild, the subordinate bird is unable to fly away. This leads to serious injuries of head, wings, and feet in the course of these confrontations. The well-known "defects of toes and claws" come about in this way. When one animal chases another around the aviary to the point of exhaustion, one must intervene and separate the animals. However, there are some instances known where the amazon pair had to "fight themselves together" before concord was attained; in this respect, the decision as to whether incompatible pairs should be split up is not all that easy.

Sometimes, "breeding pairs" are offered in advertisements. In such cases, one must make sure there is no catch, because who would sell a pair of amazons that really do breed, hatching two to four young per year? To make money, the owner could always sell the young. For a real breeding pair, the price will be considerably higher than usual. So one has to

Head of a male amazon.

Head of a female amazon.

experiment after all, during which time easily ten to fifteen birds may pass through one's hands before the ideal pair has been found.

It is an advantage if the hen is not so wild. She will then not be so easily disturbed while incubating. Skittish hens may even damage the eggs, in some instances. Under no circumstances should the cock be completely tame. He must take an active part in courtship. Tame cocks are not very ready to court, or they show little skill in copulation. It may happen that the hen will squat, but the cock will tread beside her on the branch.

Because of the psychology of the animals, pair bonding occurs in a territory equally foreign to both birds. Otherwise, one animal has the advantage of its home territory, so any others are submissive from the outset. Therefore, if one amazon is already established in the aviary, it must be removed temporarily (for about four weeks) and housed separately. The other birds bought (the female selects a mate from several males) should also be put into quarantine for about four weeks after their purchase, i.e., they should be observed to ensure that they are really healthy. During this time they can become accustomed to the air of

Above: Yellow-crowned Amazons (*A. ochrocephala ochrocephala*), 7½ months old.
Below: Yellow-crowned Amazon (*A. ochrocephala ochrocephala*), 19 days old.
Facing page: Pair of Tucuman Amazons (*A. tucumana*).

their new environment, and they can manufacture antibodies against possible agents of diseases (viruses and bacteria).

Meanwhile, the aviary is readied for breeding. All the furnishings the old bird knew and climbed on and considered its own should be replaced by new ones in different locations. Having several separate sleeping perches at the same height, one for each amazon, is important. After the end of this period, all the amazons should be put into the "new" territory at the same time. First they select a favorite perch. Since similar perches at the same height are available, no animal will feel left out. If the birds have clipped wings, the keeper should see to it that they are able to get out of each other's way by means of a system of connecting branches. It is very undesirable if some birds can fly, while others have clipped wings (except that a flighted animal is accommodating or yielding by nature). If this is the case, the space available must be very large, so that the animals can sit far enough apart. Once a pair have found one another, the other amazons must be removed again. Even in the wild, the breeding pair isolates itself from the flock. Amazons become sexually mature at about five years of age. By this age, their plumage is fully colored. However, on occasion, three-year-old hens have laid eggs. In another pair, the cock was twenty years old.

Prerequisites for Breeding The most basic prerequisite for breeding is that the animals be in perfect physical condition. Exterior appearance aside, one can recognize readiness for breeding when the amazons increasingly eat, court, and possibly screech. When sexually mature amazons—for whatever reasons—are separated from their mates and kept as single birds, they will frequently call for their mates. This is accompanied by a displacement activity: watching their reflection, which they seek in every shiny or mirrored surface. The amazon pair must have an indoor or outdoor aviary or a bird room at their disposal. There they should be completely undisturbed. As already mentioned, other amazons cannot be kept in

Rectangular nest box.

the same aviary. If there are several breeding pairs, it is an advantage if they can be kept in different places in the house or yard, so that each pair can neither see nor hear the others. This is particularly important with amazons, but perhaps not quite as applicable to cockatoos or macaws. When a pair begins courtship, they can engage in this to the fullest, without disturbing another pair which may reach this stage two to four weeks later.

Several kinds of containers have been used successfully as nest boxes for amazons: a rectangular box measuring 25 x 25 x 40 cm., a wooden keg with a capacity of 50 l. (for larger species, up to 100 l.) but especially natural tree-trunk nesting cavities. A rotting, hollow tree trunk would be ideal, but one can order nesting logs hollowed out by machine. One should select a supplier which is as nearby as possible, since the shipping costs for the log, which weighs about 50 kg., can be very high. Even though a breeding pair will not use a yardstick, but will breed in almost any space, the most common measurements for natural nesting cavities are mentioned here. For medium-sized amazons: interior diameter, 30–35 cm.; interior depth, 50–60 cm.; entrance, 9–12 cm. in diameter. An inspection door toward the bottom (10 x 10 cm.) is recommended. Underneath the entrance, a landing perch on the outside and a wire ladder on the inside should be fastened so that the animals can climb in and out without difficulties. For nesting material, peat moss, wood shavings, or sawdust can be used; sometimes the amazons will throw everything out again. To give the log a basic humidity, it is put into a tub filled with water for 24 hours. (Logs without an inspection door may be filled with water to the level of the entrance hole.) The humidity inside the nest cavity should be between 60% and 80%. It is easier to maintain this level in a nest box outdoors than in a room inside. Outdoors, the log, which must not hang in direct sunlight, can be sprayed, on hot days only; indoors, one has to be concerned constantly about increasing humidity. There are electric humidifiers for this purpose. The amazons absorb some moisture with their feathers when they are being sprayed and thereby they themselves contribute to a humid climate inside the breeding cavity. However, one should not overdo the moisture. It is unhealthy for an amazon hen to sit where it is damp; also, fungi are likely to grow. If the aviary has both a flight and a shelter room, make two nesting

Nest box made from a log.

sites available, one inside and out.

The food offered must be very diverse during the breeding season and especially must contain a lot of protein. One should offer sprouts, fruit, rose hips, chickweed, cooked fish, yogurt, or wheat grits with egg; or mix a moist, crumbly mass from zwieback, hard-boiled egg, vitamin drops, and baby food (see the sections on feeding and on particular species).

The Breeding Cycle Most often a breeding pair becomes active with the beginning of spring. They inspect the nesting cavity; the cock feeds his hen more frequently. The feeding ritual prepares him for his later duty of providing the incubating female and the young with food. During courtship, a sort of "dress rehearsal" takes place. At the same time, courtship displays occur more often, in the course of which the animals parade up and down with wings spread and tails fanned. The pupils are narrowed and the neck feathers puffed up, as specific sounds are made. It has been observed on occasion that the male presented the female with a twig as a "wedding present." The actual treading, which lasts for several minutes, follows, during which the cock mounts the hen from the side, holding on to her back with beak and claws, and presses his vent against hers. According to R. Low, sometimes treading is facilitated if there is a flat surface available, such as a board, in addition to the usual perches.

Amazons do not like to be observed. Therefore, one should install a small peephole in one wall of the aviary, through which one can watch, undetected by the birds. Their behavior will be completely different from what it is when the keeper is in the aviary. That egg laying has begun will be evident from the very long disappearances of the hen into the nest box. The animals should not be disturbed unnecessarily now; nor will the cock allow it. He will be so aggressive that it is almost impossible to enter his territory. Even formerly tame amazons become unpredictable.

Since infertile eggs are often laid, possible causes should be considered: It could be that

White-fronted Amazon *(A. albifrons)*. On the male (above, left) the alula and primary coverts are red, and there is more red around the eye than in the female (above, right), which has the alula and primary coverts green.
Below: Youngster at 10 weeks of age.

Facing page: *1*. Wing of male. *2*. Head of male. *3*. Wing of female. *4*. Eggs. *5*. Nestling at 14 days. *6*. Deformed foot, probably caused by nutritional deficiency in the food offered the parents. *7*. Underdeveloped wing; both defects could be ameliorated by vitamin supplements. *8*. Nestling at 21 days. *9*. 28 days. *10*. 42 days. *11*. 56 days. *12*. Parents warning the youngster off.

the cock is still too young. With older cocks, it can happen that they are not in the mood to breed, though the hen lays one egg after another. Or the cock may simply be too fat. For fertilized eggs that do not hatch, the following explanations may apply: the eggs chilled during a too-long interruption of incubation; the diet was inadequate; the temperature and humidity were too low; the eggs got cracked, perhaps by the leg band of the hen.

Usually, eggs are laid at two-day intervals. Only the female incubates. The cock may enter the nest box to feed, once the hen sits firmly— on the third day at the earliest. Usually, the hen leaves the nest box once a day for a short time: at first to eat and later to be fed; and, of course, for evacuation. (The droppings excreted during the breeding period are improbably large; to some extent they are the waste of more than one day.) Finally, the hen will bathe, because the wet plumage increases the humidity inside the box.

The incubation period lasts about four weeks. During this time, the animals are, as mentioned already, extremely aggressive. They are dangerous to the bird keeper if he enters the aviary. Cleaning is often impossible, and it is wise if the food can be supplied from outside. Formerly tame birds are the most dangerous, since they are not afraid of people and use their beaks ruthlessly. The young hatch blind, with only a few down feathers. Nest inspection at this period of time is extremely risky, because the disturbance may cause the parents to stop tending their young. If there are still eggs in the nest cavity after the calculated date of hatching, one should not check immediately and open them; instead, leave them to be incubated for another week, and only then remove the clutch. The mother does not always remain in the nest box until the young are ready to leave. She and the cock will sleep

outside again. In such a situation, nest inspection can be done at night.

Like all South American parrots (as opposed to the Australian), the amazon chicks remain in the nest a comparatively long time. Their nestling period lasts about seventy days. At about four weeks, their eyes are completely open. Their bodies are now thickly covered with gray down. At the age of six weeks, the fuzz takes on a green hue, and yellow, red, blue, or white markings are just noticeable. Feathers begin to sprout everywhere. At ten weeks, the young animals are covered with feathers. If the cavity in the nesting log has a wire ladder on the inside, which the young can climb up, they will come out sooner. After their first flight out, they should be put back into the nesting cavity in the evening, so that they are not deprived of their security too soon. When they come out the second time, they are grown-up enough to orient themselves outside.

The cock continues to provide the young with food regularly, even though they already take soft foods by themselves. The hen is no longer the faithfully caring mother now, as she was during the nestling period. On the other hand, at times it has been observed that the hen continued to feed the young and the cock chased them off. In any case, at three to four months the young become so self-sufficient that they can feed themselves. From the older animals they learn how seeds are eaten. Now they can be separated from their parents. Of course, if biting occurs, they should be removed earlier.

These are the points of amazon breeding that can be generalized. Further details can be found in the species sections that follow. If any readers have themselves bred amazons and would like to tell about it, the authors are interested in their reports. Letters may be sent in the care of the publisher.

Species and Subspecies

General The origin of the different species and subspecies is explained by the theory of evolution. In the course of millennia, animals which are separated by geographical circumstances, such as mountains, islands, and similar spatial factors, continue to evolve into separate populations. The later the separation took place, the more closely related are the animals, and the closer is their resemblance in exterior appearance.

Species denotes the natural, procreative communities in which genes are exchanged through mating. The individuals of a species are among themselves one hundred-percent fertile. Even if the range of a species extends over wide distances and subspecies have arisen, these may interbreed in the areas where they come into contact. Thus subspecies are not isolated procreatively, but often spatially or even in time, e.g., by different phases of activity. Subspecies may be differentiated by divergences in coloration or in vocal utterances.

Thus, for instance, the Tucuman Amazon (*Amazona tucumana*) and the Red-spectacled Amazon (*Amazona pretrei*) were for a time considered subspecies of the same species. Then it was discovered that both forms occurred in Misiones (northeastern Argentina) *without* interbreeding. Evidently, courtship went awry, or partially awry, with the consequence that the animals did not recognize each other as sex partners. It follows from this that they are two distinct species. (Dr. Wolters has indicated that there have been no recent reports of the Tucuman Amazon from Misiones. If, however, hybrids of the two forms should regularly be found somewhere in the wild, one would have to assume that the Tucuman and the Red-spectacled belong together as the same species.)

Hybridization in captivity is another matter. If a suitable sex partner of its own species is lacking, a parrot will mate out of necessity with another of a different species. Such bastards do not occur in nature, because this mixing would run contrary to evolution. If offspring are raised in captivity from a crossing of different species, they are not always fertile. It appears that the offspring are proportionately less fertile when the relationship between the parent animals is more distant.

Systematics This book follows the systematics of Wolters (1975); at present (1981), he still adheres to this listing. According to it, the order of Parrots (Psittaciformes) is divided into twelve families. To the family of "New World Parrots" (Aratingidae) belong all American parrots. One of the six subfamilies of the New World Parrots are the "Amazonlike Parrots" (Amazoninae). The Amazonlike Parrots are divided, in turn, into eight genera, one of which is the genus of Amazon Parrots (*Amazona*); this name was introduced in 1830 by Lesson. The Amazon Parrots are twenty-nine species, or, to be exact, twenty-seven living and two extinct species of amazons. Some authors arrive at only twenty-six species; they list the Tucuman Amazon (*Amazona tucumana*) together with the Red-spectacled Amazon (*Amazona pretrei*) as a single species (*Amazona pretrei pretrei; Amazona pretrei tucumana*). Wolters excludes conspecificity in this instance, but in another case he suggests the possibility that the Red-tailed Amazon (*Amazona brasiliensis*) and the Blue-cheeked Amazon (*Amazona dufresniana*) may be the same species. Also, the Imperial Amazon (*Amazona imperialis*) and the extinct *Amazona violacea* may, according to Wolters, belong to the same species. However, he indicates the conspecificity in both instances with a question mark and lists them as separate species.

Sequence of Species The sequence of the amazon species given here follows that of

Wolters. The species are ordered in such a manner that the subgenera proposed, so far as can be ascertained today, are holophyletic and that similar subgenera are in every case placed next to one another, to the extent that our incomplete insight into their phylogenetic relationships allows.

Order				
Psittaciformes (Parrots)	▶ **Family**			
	Aratingidae ("New World Parrots")	▶ **Subfamily**		
	Psittacidae ("Grey Parrots")	Forpinae ("Sparrow Parrots")		
	Psittaculidae ("Noble Parrots")	Aratinginae ("Wedge-tailed Parakeets")		
	Loriculidae ("Bat Parrots")	Brotogeryinae ("Small-billed Parrots")		
	Psittrichadidae ("Bristle-heads")	Amazoninae ("Amazonlike Parrots")	▶ **Genus**	
	Loriidae (Lories)	Triclariinae ("Parakeet Parrots")	*Touit* ("Colored-tailed Parrots")	
	Platycercidae ("Broad-tailed Parakeets")	Pionitinae ("White-bellied Parrots")	*Gypopsitta* ("Bare-headed Parrots")	
	Melopsittacidae (Budgerigars)		*Hapalopsittaca* ("Brown-eared Parrots")	
	Pezoporidae ("Ground Parakeets")		*Pionopsitta* ("Ornamental Parrots")	
	Strigopidae ("Owl Parrots")		*Graydidascalus* (Short-tailed Parrots)	
	Nestoridae ("Nestor Parrots")		*Amazona* (Amazon Parrots)	▶
	Cacatuidae (Cockatoos)		*Deroptyus* ("Fan Parrots")	
			Pionus ("Red-vented Parrots")	

The ordering of the races within a species is done according to Forshaw, since Wolters makes no statement about this. For the sake of completeness and for the information of the reader, two amazon subspecies under dispute (according to R. Low, 1980) are included: a small form of the Orange-winged Amazon (*Amazona amazonica micra*) and a large form of the Double Yellow-headed Amazon (*Amazona ochrocephala magna*). For Forshaw, the small Orange-winged Amazon is not separable from the nominate form (*Amazona amazonica amazonica*), nor the larger Double Yellow-headed Amazon from *Amazona ochrocephala oratrix*.

The following four sequences of the amazon species show how Wolters, Forshaw, de Grahl, and Low have listed them. For the sake of clarity, only the scientific name of the species is given.

* = doubtful subspecies
† = extinct
[= subgenera

Species (29, incl. 2 extinct)	Subspecies (incl. 1 extinct)
A. festiva (Festive Amazon)	*f. festiva* *f. bodini*
A. tucumana (Tucuman Amazon)	
A. pretrei (Red-spectacled Amazon)	
A. agilis (Black-billed Amazon)	
A. vittata (Puerto Rican Amazon)	*v. vittata* *v. gracilipes*†
A. albifrons (White-fronted Amazon)	*a. albifrons* *a. saltuensis* *a. nana*
A. xantholora (Yellow-lored Amazon)	
A. ventralis (Hispaniolan Amazon)	
A. leucocephala (Cuban Amazon)	*l. leucocephala* *l. palmarum* *l. caymanensis* *l. hesterna* *l. bahamensis*
A. collaria (Yellow-billed Amazon)	
A. xanthops (Yellow-faced Amazon)	
A. finschi (Lilac-crowned Amazon)	*f. finschi* *f. woodi*
A. viridigenalis (Green-cheeked Amazon)	
A. autumnalis (Red-lored Amazon)	*a. autumnalis* *a. salvini* *a. lilacina* *a. diadema*
A. brasiliensis (Red-tailed Amazon)	
A. dufresniana (Blue-cheeked Amazon)	*d. dufresniana* *d. rhodocorytha*
A. mercenaria (Scaly-naped Amazon)	*m. mercenaria* *m. canipalliata*
A. amazonica (Orange-winged Amazon)	*a. amazonica* *a. tobagensis* *a. micra**
A. barbadensis (Yellow-shouldered Amazon)	*b. barbadensis* *b. rothschildi*
A. aestiva (Blue-fronted Amazon)	*a. aestiva* *a. xanthopteryx*
A. ochrocephala (Yellow-crowned Amazon)	*o. ochrocephala* *o. xantholaema* *o. nattereri* *o. panamensis* *o. auropalliata* *o. parvipes* *o. belizensis* *o. oratrix* *o. tresmariae* *o. magna**
A. farinosa (Mealy Amazon)	*f. farinosa* *f. inornata* *f. chapmani* *f. ventriceps* *f. guatemalae*
A. arausiaca (Red-necked Amazon)	
A. versicolor (St. Lucia Amazon)	
A. guildingii (St. Vincent Amazon)	
A. martinica† (Martinique Amazon)	
A. imperialis (Imperial Amazon)	
A. violacea† (Violet Amazon)	
A. vinacea (Vinaceous Amazon)	

Yellow-crowned Amazon (*A. ochrocephala*).   **Red-lored Amazon (*A. autumnalis*)**

	Wolters (1975)	Forshaw (1978)	de Grahl (1974)	Low (1980)
1.	festiva	collaria	collaria	agilis
2.	tucumana	leucocephala	leucocephala	collaria
3.	pretrei	ventralis	ventralis	leucocephala
4.	agilis	albifrons	xantholora	ventralis
5.	vittata	xantholora	albifrons	albifrons[1]
6.	albifrons	agilis	agilis	vittata
7.	xantholora	vittata	vittata	pretrei[2]
8.	ventralis	tucumana	pretrei[2]	viridigenalis
9.	leucocephala	pretrei	viridigenalis	finschi
10.	collaria	viridigenalis	finschi	autumnalis
11.	xanthops	finschi	autumnalis	dufresniana
12.	finschi	autumnalis	dufresniana	brasiliensis
13.	viridigenalis	brasiliensis	brasiliensis	festiva
14.	autumnalis	dufresniana	arausiaca	xanthops
15.	brasiliensis	festiva	festiva	barbadensis
16.	dufresniana	xanthops	xanthops	aestiva
17.	mercenaria	barbadensis	barbadensis	amazonica
18.	amazonica	aestiva	aestiva	ochrocephala
19.	barbadensis	ochrocephala	ochrocephala	mercenaria
20.	aestiva	amazonica	amazonica	farinosa
21.	ochrocephala	mercenaria	mercenaria	vinacea
22.	farinosa	farinosa ·	farinosa	guildingii
23.	arausiaca	vinacea	vinacea	versicolor
24.	versicolor	versicolor	guildingii	imperialis
25.	guildingii	arausiaca	versicolor	arausiaca
26.	martinica†	guildingii	imperialis	*
27.	imperialis	imperialis	*	*
28.	violacea†	*	*	
29.	vinacea	*		

[1] = including *xantholora*
[2] = including *tucumana*
† = extinct
* = extinct species omitted

NAMES To facilitate the reader's acquaintance with the scientific names, here are two lists of the names of the amazons: the first lists the scientific names alphabetically; the second, the English names. [English names of species, following Forshaw, are boldfaced. Names in quotation marks are literal translations of the German names. — *Ed.*]

1. SCIENTIFIC NAMES

A. aestiva aestiva: **Blue-fronted**, Turquoise-fronted, "Red-bend"

A. aestiva xanthopteryx: Yellow-winged, "Yellow-winged Blue-fronted"

A. agilis: **Black-billed**, Active, All-green, "Red-speculum"

A. albifrons: **White-fronted**, Spectacled, White-browed, Red-White-and-Blue

A. amazonica: **Orange-winged**

A. arausiaca: **Red-necked**, Blue-faced Dominican, Bouquet's, "Blue-headed"

A. autumnalis autumnalis: **Red-lored**, Scarlet-lored, Primrose-cheeked, Yellow-cheeked, Orange-cheeked, "Red-fronted," "Autumnal"

A. autumnalis diadema: Diademed, "Red-fronted"

A. autumnalis lilacina: Lilacine, Lesson's, "Red-fronted"

A. autumnalis salvini: Salvin's, "Red-fronted"

A. barbadensis barbadensis: **Yellow-shouldered**, "Yellow-winged," "Sun Parrot," "Smaller Yellow-headed"

A. barbadensis rothschildi: Rothschild's, "Yellow-winged," "Sun Parrot," "Smaller Yellow-headed"

A. brasiliensis: **Red-tailed**, Brazilian Green, Blue-faced, "Red-masked"

A. collaria: **Yellow-billed**, Red-throated, Jamaican

A. dufresniana dufresniana: **Blue-cheeked**, Dufresne's, "Red-crowned"

A. dufresniana rhodocorytha: Red-crowned, Red-browed, Red-capped, Red-topped, "Blue-cheeked"

A. farinosa chapmani: "Mealy"

A. farinosa farinosa: **Mealy**

A. farinosa guatemalae: Blue-crowned, Guatemalan, "Mealy"

A. farinosa inornata: Plain-colored, "Mealy"

A. farinosa virenticeps: Green-headed, Costa Rican, "Mealy"

A. festiva bodini: Bodin's, "Red-fronted"

A. festiva festiva: **Festive**, Red-backed, "Blue-bearded," "Blue-chinned"

A. finschi finschi: **Lilac-crowned**, Finsch's, "Blue-capped"

A. finschi woodi: Wood's Lilac-crowned, "Blue-capped"

A. guildingii: **St. Vincent**, Guilding's, "Royal"

A. imperialis: **Imperial**, August, "Emperor," "Brown-tailed"

A. leucocephala bahamensis: Bahaman, "White-headed"

A. leucocephala caymanensis: Grand Cayman, "White-headed"

A. leucocephala hesterna: Cayman Brac, Little Cayman, "White-headed"

A. leucocephala leucocephala: **Cuban**, "White-headed"

A. leucocephala palmarum: Isle of Pines, "White-headed"

A. martinica†: **Martinique**

A. mercenaria canipalliata: Grey-naped, Tschudi's, Colombian, "Orange-winged"

A. mercenaria mercenaria: **Scaly-naped**, Mercenary, "Soldierly"

A. ochrocephala auropalliata: Yellow-naped, Golden-naped, Panama Parrot

A. ochrocephala belizensis: "Double Yellow-headed," "Greater Yellow-headed"

A. ochrocephala magna: "Double Yellow-headed," "Greater Yellow-headed"

A. ochrocephala nattereri: Natterer's, "Green"

A. ochrocephala ochrocephala: **Yellow-crowned**, Yellow-fronted, Single Yellow-headed, Yellow-headed, Colombian

A. ochrocephala oratrix: Yellow-headed, Double Yellow-headed, Mexican Yellow-headed, Levaillant's, Double Yellow-fronted, "Greater Yellow-headed"

A. ochrocephala panamensis: Panama Amazon, "Yellow-fronted"

A. ochrocephala parvipes: "Yellow-naped"

A. ochrocephala tresmariae: Tres Marias, "Double Yellow-headed, "Greater Yellow-headed"

A. ochrocephala xantholaema: Marajo

A. pretrei: **Red-spectacled**, Pretre's, "Splendid," "Red-flecked"

A. tucumana: **Tucuman**

A. ventralis: **Hispaniolan**, Santo Domingo, Salle's, White-headed, "Blue-crowned"

A. versicolor: **St. Lucia**, Versicolor, Blue-masked, "Blue-fronted"

A. vinacea: **Vinaceous**, "Pigeon-necked," "Wine-red," "Blue-throated"

A. violacea†: **Violet**

A. viridigenalis: **Green-cheeked**, Red-crowned, Mexican Red-headed, "Red-masked"

A. vittata gracilipes†: Culebran

A. vittata vittata: **Puerto Rican**, Red-fronted

A. xantholora: **Yellow-lored**, "Golden-lored"

A. xanthops: **Yellow-faced**, Yellow-crowned, "Yellow-bellied," "Golden-bellied"

2. ENGLISH NAMES

Active	*A. agilis*
All-green	*A. agilis*
August	*A. imperialis*
Bahaman	*A. leucocephala bahamensis*
Black-billed	*A. agilis*
Blue-cheeked	*A. dufresniana dufresniana*
Blue-crowned	*A. farinosa guatemalae*
Blue-faced	*A. brasiliensis*
Blue-faced Dominican	*A. arausiaca*
Blue-fronted	*A. aestiva aestiva*
Blue-masked	*A. versicolor*
Bodin's	*A. festiva bodini*
Bouquet's	*A. arausiaca*
Brazilian Green	*A. brasiliensis*
Cayman Brac	*A. leucocephala hesterna*
Colombian	*A. ochrocephala ochrocephala*
Costa Rican	*A. farinosa virenticeps*
Cuban	*A. leucocephala leucocephala*
Culebran†	*A. vittata gracilipes*
Diademed	*A. autumnalis diadema*
Double Yellow-fronted	*A. ochrocephala oratrix*
Double Yellow-headed	*A. ochrocephala oratrix*
Dufresne's	*A. dufresniana dufresniana*
Festive	*A. festiva festiva*
Finsch's	*A. finschi finschi*
Golden-naped	*A. ochrocephala auropalliata*
Grand Cayman	*A. leucocephala caymanensis*
Green-cheeked	*A. viridigenalis*
Green-headed	*A. farinosa virenticeps*
Grey-naped	*A. mercenaria canipalliata*
Guilding's	*A. guildingii*
Guatemalan	*A. farinosa guatemalae*
Hispaniolan	*A. ventralis*
Imperial	*A. imperialis*
Isle of Pines	*A. leucocephala palmarum*
Jamaican	*A. collaria*
Lesson's	*A. autumnalis lilacina*
Levaillant's	*A. ochrocephala oratrix*
Lilac-crowned	*A. finschi finschi*
Lilacine	*A. autumnalis lilacina*
Little Cayman	*A. leucocephala hesterna*
Marajo	*A. ochrocephala xantholaema*
Martinique†	*A. martinica*
Mealy	*A. farinosa farinosa*
Mercenary	*A. mercenaria mercenaria*
Mexican Red-headed	*A. viridigenalis*
Mexican Yellow-headed	*A. ochrocephala oratrix*
Natterer's	*A. ochrocephala nattereri*
Orange-cheeked	*A. autumnalis autumnalis*
Orange-winged	*A. amazonica*
Panama Amazon	*A. ochrocephala panamensis*
Panama Parrot	*A. ochrocephala auropalliata*
Plain-colored	*A. farinosa inornata*
Pretre's	*A. pretrei*
Primrose-cheeked	*A. autumnalis autumnalis*
Puerto Rican	*A. vittata vittata*
Red-backed	*A. festiva festiva*
Red-browed	*A. dufresniana rhodocorytha*
Red-capped	*A. dufresniana rhodocorytha*
Red-crowned	*A. dufresniana rhodocorytha*
Red-crowned	*A. viridigenalis*
Red-fronted	*A. vittata vittata*
Red-lored	*A. autumnalis autumnalis*
Red-necked	*A. arausiaca*
Red-spectacled	*A. pretrei*
Red-tailed	*A. brasiliensis*
Red-throated	*A. collaria*
Red-topped	*A. dufresniana rhodocorytha*
Red-White-and-Blue	*A. albifrons*
Rothschild's	*A. barbadensis rothschildi*
Salle's	*A. ventralis*
Salvin's	*A. autumnalis salvini*
Santo Domingo	*A. ventralis*
Scaly-naped	*A. mercenaria mercenaria*
Scarlet-lored	*A. autumnalis autumnalis*
Single Yellow-headed	*A. ochrocephala ochrocephala*
Spectacled	*A. albifrons*
St. Lucia	*A. versicolor*
St. Vincent	*A. guildingii*
Tres Marias	*A. ochrocephala tresmariae*
Tschudi's	*A. mercenaria canipalliata*
Tucuman	*A. tucumana*
Turquoise-fronted	*A. aestiva aestiva*
Versicolor	*A. versicolor*
Vinaceous	*A. vinacea*
Violet†	*A. violacea*
White-browed	*A. albifrons*
White-fronted	*A. albifrons*
White-headed	*A. ventralis*
Wood's Lilac-crowned	*A. finschi woodi*
Yellow-billed	*A. collaria*
Yellow-cheeked	*A. autumnalis autumnalis*
Yellow-crowned	*A. ochrocephala ochrocephala*
Yellow-crowned	*A. xanthops*
Yellow-faced	*A. xanthops*
Yellow-fronted	*A. ochrocephala ochrocephala*
Yellow-headed	*A. ochrocephala ochrocephala*
Yellow-lored	*A. xantholora*
Yellow-naped	*A. ochrocephala auropalliata*
Yellow-shouldered	*A. barbadensis barbadensis*
Yellow-winged	*A. aestiva xanthopteryx*

Plumage Nomenclature

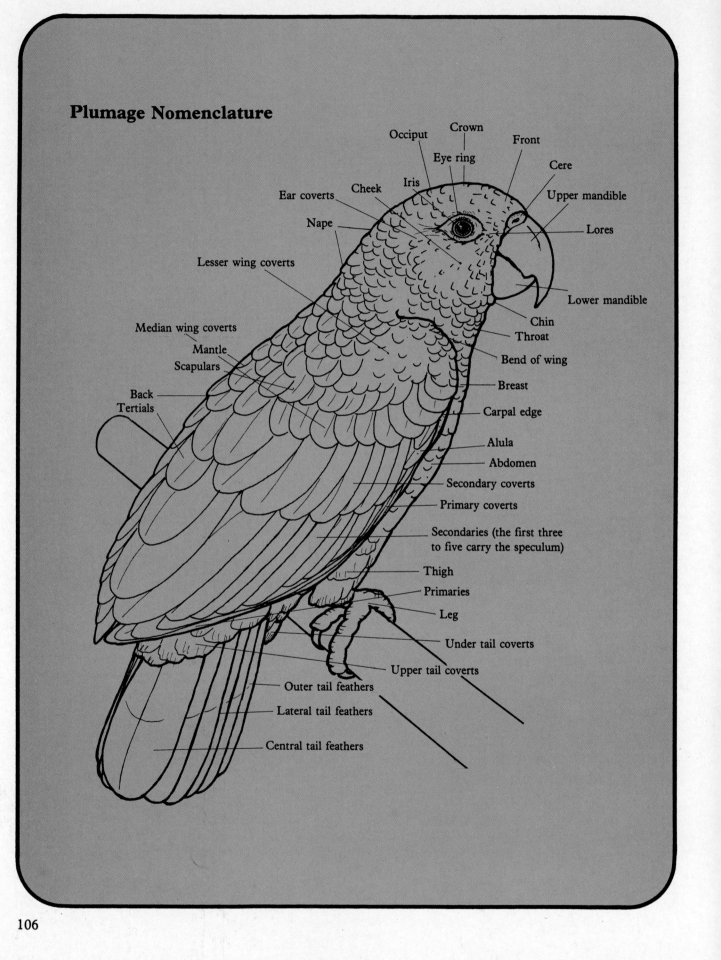

Occiput · Crown · Front · Cere · Eye ring · Upper mandible · Iris · Ear coverts · Cheek · Lores · Nape · Lower mandible · Lesser wing coverts · Chin · Throat · Bend of wing · Median wing coverts · Breast · Mantle · Scapulars · Carpal edge · Back · Tertials · Alula · Abdomen · Secondary coverts · Primary coverts · Secondaries (the first three to five carry the speculum) · Thigh · Primaries · Leg · Under tail coverts · Upper tail coverts · Outer tail feathers · Lateral tail feathers · Central tail feathers

For the sake of better orientation, the amazon species and subspecies are ordered to a decimal system of classification. In the sequence according to Wolters, the species are given the numbers 1–29.

3. NUMERICAL SEQUENCE

1.	Festive Amazon	*A. festiva*
2.	Tucuman Amazon	*A. tucumana*
3.	Red-spectacled Amazon	*A. pretrei*
4.	Black-billed Amazon	*A. agilis*
5.	Puerto Rican Amazon	*A. vittata*
6.	White-fronted Amazon	*A. albifrons*
7.	Yellow-lored Amazon	*A. xantholora*
8.	Hispaniolan Amazon	*A. ventralis*
9.	Cuban Amazon	*A. leucocephala*
10.	Yellow-billed Amazon	*A. collaria*
11.	Yellow-faced Amazon	*A. xanthops*
12.	Lilac-crowned Amazon	*A. finschi*
13.	Green-cheeked Amazon	*A. viridigenalis*
14.	Red-lored Amazon	*A. autumnalis*
15.	Red-tailed Amazon	*A. brasiliensis*
16.	Blue-cheeked Amazon	*A. dufresniana*
17.	Scaly-naped Amazon	*A. mercenaria*
18.	Orange-winged Amazon	*A. amazonica*
19.	Yellow-shouldered Amazon	*A. barbadensis*
20.	Blue-fronted Amazon	*A. aestiva*
21.	Yellow-crowned Amazon	*A. ochrocephala*
22.	Mealy Amazon	*A. farinosa*
23.	Red-necked Amazon	*A. arausiaca*
24.	St. Lucia Amazon	*A. versicolor*
25.	St. Vincent Amazon	*A. guildingii*
26.	Martinique Amazon	*A. martinica*†
27.	Imperial Amazon	*A. imperialis*
28.	Violet Amazon	*A. violacea*†
29.	Vinaceous Amazon	*A. vinacea*

After the English name of the species, the subspecies are indicated by numbers following the decimal point. For example, Red-lored Amazon, 14.1 = *Amazona autumnalis autumnalis*, the nominate form; 14.2 = *Amazona autumnalis salvini*; 14.3 = *Amazona autumnalis lilacina*; and 14.4 = *Amazona autumnalis diadema*.

The sign ‡ preceding the scientific names indicates that the subspecies is protected under the Washington Convention [Convention on International Trade in Endangered Species of Wild Flora and Fauna (CITES)]. The sign †

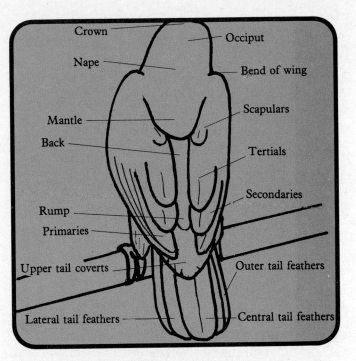

Back view of an amazon.

means that the species is extinct.

Following the scientific name of the subspecies is the name of the person who first described the subspecies, and the year. Parentheses enclosing the person's name show that the current scientific name is no longer the same as the name given it by the describer.

Wing viewed from above.

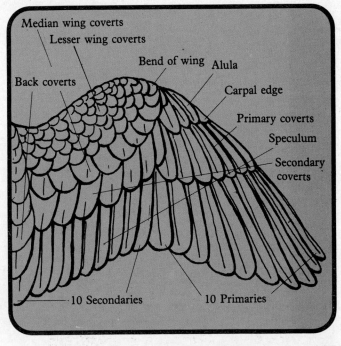

Plumage Nomenclature The descriptions of the species and subspecies always follow the same sequence. If particular parts of the plumage are omitted, it should be understood that they are colored green. For the subspecies, only parts that differ from the nominate form are mentioned; the parts not listed can be found under the nominate form.

If the literature provides differing reports about some character, the following authors are indicated by abbreviations:

(F) = Forshaw
(G) = de Grahl
(L) = Low
(P) = Pinter

The names of other authors, which occur less frequently, are written out in full.

In the following descriptions of the species and races, constantly recurring terms will be used. A better understanding of the parts of the plumage can be obtained from the three drawings shown. *Wing speculum* indicates the first three to five secondaries when they differ notably in coloration from the others.

Differences in Talking Ability In the descriptions of the species and subspecies, talent for talking is discussed as far as there is relevant information about it in the literature. Apparently, some species more than others produce individuals with a talent for speech. We believe that such evaluations should be met skeptically. Often, the frequently imported amazons are said to be talented talkers, whereas rare species are considered untalented in this respect. Naturally, one will find among a thousand keepers of Panama Yellow-crowned Amazons (*Amazona ochrocephala panamensis*) more positive reports about the talents of these birds than among ten keepers of Vinaceous Amazons (*Amazona vinacea*). The conclusion might be drawn, hastily, that Panama Yellow-crowned Amazons are better at talking than Vinaceous Amazons; however, this is not necessarily true. Pinter (1979) writes that the Vinaceous Amazons are among the best talkers, while de Grahl ascribes to the "average bird"

no very great talent. Yet he does remark that over and over again very different reports are made about any given species. R. Low quotes, among others, a report by S. Porter, who describes the Vinaceous Amazon as an extremely quiet bird. She adds that the reader should not be misled into believing that this is a quiet species of amazon – no, it is just as noisy as the others. The remarks made in this book about the talent for talking should be taken in this light. If a reader should read a negative comment about the talking ability of his amazon, he must not lose patience with the animal too quickly. In his case, the contrary may apply. Every individual animal has its particular talent.

FESTIVE AMAZON

1.1 *Amazona festiva festiva* (Linné) 1758

Range: From eastern Ecuador, northwest Peru, and southeastern Colombia eastward through the Amazon basin to the Madeira in Brazil

Description:
Length: 34–35 cm.
Basic color: Green, neck feathers edged pale black
Forehead: Narrow band of dark-red
Occiput: Sometimes blue
Lores: Dark red
Eye region: Blue above and behind the eyes
Cheeks: Bright yellow-green
Chin: Blue (light)
Carpal edge: Pale yellow-green
Primaries: Purple-blue, narrowly edged yellow-green
Primary coverts: Purple-blue, narrowly edged green
Secondaries: Narrowly edged yellow-green
Back and rump: Scarlet red

1.1 *festiva festiva*

Breeding: No pure breeding in captivity is known. Low mentions a crossing with a female Yellow-billed Amazon (*Amazona collaria*), which produced three young. Wolters mentions a crossing with a Blue-fronted Amazon (*Amazona aestiva*). According to Bedford, Canon Dutton owned a yellow specimen, probably not a lutino, as it did not have red eyes and pale legs.

Remarks: The talent for talking is considerable (G), and there are even excellent talkers (Bedford). Some are better at imitating noises rather than the human voice (P). They are quickly tamed and then become lovable companions. They are rarely found in the trade.

Tail: Green with yellow-green tips, outer vanes of lateral tail feathers edged with blue (L); bases of inner vanes red (G)
Under tail coverts: Yellow-green
Beak: Gray to black
Cere: Blue-gray
Eye ring: Blue-gray
Iris: Orange-red
Legs: Pale gray-green (F)

Sex-related differences: None

Young: Paler and less extensive blue above and behind the eyes, on chin and occiput; back and rump green with single red feathers, some lateral tail feathers with red at the base (F)

Life in the wild: Festive Amazons love the forests along the riverbanks. They occur along the upper Amazon and its tributaries, but are also found in other areas. Dr. J. Steinbacher reports in the November 1978 issue of *Die Gefiederte Welt* about his travels through Ecuador. As only ten percent of the light finds it way through the leafy canopy of the giant trees, the faunas live in the treetops. *Amazona festiva* was observed in small groups in clearings.

1.2 *Amazona festiva bodini* (Finsch)

Range: Venezuela, in the vicinity of the central Orinoco from the river Meta to the Delta Amacuro; northwest Guyana, along the Barima river

1.2 *festiva bodini*

Festive Amazon (*A. festiva festiva*). Its most
notable characteristic is the red on its back.

Tucuman Amazon (*A. tucumana*). Normally the front is a brighter red.

Description:
Basic color: Yellowish green, particularly ventrally
Forehead: Red extends to the crown
Crown and occiput: Feathers partly edged with dull red
Nape: Strongly dark edging
Lores: Blackish (F, G); red (P)
Cheeks: Blue-green, violet-blue edging
Carpal edge: Yellow
Primaries: Outer vanes green
Primary coverts: Green
Back: Carmine red (L)
Eye ring: Blackish

Young: Back still green

Remarks: Hopkinson describes an intermediary species between *Amazona festiva festiva* and *Amazona festiva bodini* (L). It has no blue cheeks, but does have black-edged nape feathers. So far unexplained, it could be seen in the collection of H. Whitley.

The talent for talking is moderate; the birds are better at imitating animal (e.g., dog and cat) sounds (L). They become very tame and affectionate (G).

2 *tucumana*

Primaries: Green, becoming blue toward the tips
Primary coverts: Red
Secondaries: The outermost feathers have blue outer vanes; those toward the inside are blue, and green toward their bases
Secondary coverts: Red
Underside of the flight feathers: Olive-green
Tail: Green with yellow-green tips
Tail coverts: Yellow-green
Beak: Yellow-gray (P); horn-colored (F)
Cere: Light gray
Eye ring: White
Iris: Yellow-orange
Legs: Reddish light gray

Sex-related differences: None

Young: Thighs green

Life in the Wild: The Tucuman Amazon prefers alder forests. It occurs predominantly along the eastern slope of the Andes to an elevation of 2000 m., as well as in the hills at the foot of the Andes. It is also found in northeast Argentina, where, however, no nesting sites have been discovered.

Breeding: In Bolivia breeding takes place in January. On the average, four eggs are laid. Breeding in captivity has not been reported.

TUCUMAN AMAZON

2. *Amazona tucumana* (Cabanis) 1885

Range: Southeastern Bolivia in the vicinity of Chuquisaca and Tarija; northern Argentina from Jujuy eastward to Misiones

Description:
Length: 31 cm.
Basic color: Dark green; feathers on head, neck, breast, and abdomen strongly black edged
Forehead: Red
Crown: Red in front
Cheeks: Sides of the head bluish (G)
Thighs: Orange

Remarks: These amazons are hardly ever exported to Europe; they are said to be very shy in the wild.

RED-SPECTACLED AMAZON

3. *Amazona pretrei*
‡ (Temminck) 1830

Range: Southeastern part of Brazil (from São Paulo to Rio Grande); northeastern Argentina (Misiones); occasionally in the north of Uruguay and the extreme southeast of Paraguay.

Description:
Length: 31–32 cm.
Basic color: Green, paler and lighter on head, neck, and underside; feather edging black
Forehead: Red
Crown: Red
Lores: Red
Eye region: Red
Thighs: Red
Bend of wing: Red

3 pretrei

Carpal edge and alula: Red
Primaries: Green with blue at the tips (F); red (G, P)
Primary coverts: Red
Secondaries: Green, shading toward blue at the tips
Tail: Green with wide yellow-green tips, the three outermost having red spots on the bases of the inner vanes.
Tail coverts: Yellow-green
Beak: Yellowish horn-colored; upper mandible orange at the base (L)
Cere: Pale horn-colored
Eye ring: White
Iris: Orange-yellow
Legs: Pale yellow-brown (F); greyish (G)

Sex-related differences: None

Young: Eye area green with single red feathers, carpal edge green

Life in the Wild: Red-spectacled Amazons prefer *Araucaria* forests and like to eat the seeds of these trees; they have been observed eating together with Vinaceous Amazons (*Amazona vinacea*), and sometimes form mixed flocks with the Red-tailed Amazon (*Amazona brasiliensis*). The number of Red-spectacled Amazons has decreased because of the clearing of the forests, but apparently the survival of the species is not directly endangered.

Breeding: Presumably, the breeding takes place in October (F); nothing else is known.

BLACK-BILLED AMAZON

4. *Amazona agilis*
(Linné) 1758

Range: Jamaica

Description:
Length: 25 cm.

The Red-spectacled Amazon (*A. pretrei*) is sometimes treated as a subspecies of the Tucuman Amazon (*A. tucumana*).

**The Black-billed Amazon (*A. agilis*) sometimes has
a red spot on the lores.**

Basic color: Dark green; underside paler, yellowish
Forehead: Most have a few red feathers
Crown: Top of head blue-green (G)
Nape: Edged blackish
Ear coverts: Sometimes blackish (G)
Primaries: Dark blue-purple
Primary coverts: Outer ones red
Secondaries: Dark blue, green toward the base
Wing speculum: Small light-red spot (G)
Underside of flight feathers: Blue-green
Under wing coverts: Blue-green
Tail: Central feathers green; lateral feathers have red spots on the bases of the inner vanes (F); inner vanes yellow with red spot (G); outer vanes have blue cast
Under tail coverts: Yellow-green
Beak: Gray, tip of upper mandible darker
Cere: Dark gray
Eye ring: Dark gray
Iris: Dark brown
Legs: Dark green-gray

Sex-related differences: *Female:* no red in the primary coverts (not certainly proven – L); some primary coverts green instead of red (F)

Young: Primary coverts green; top of head green, iris black (G)

4 agilis

Life in the wild: They live in moderate humidity in the linden forests of Mount Diablo and the "Cockpit Country." Formerly, they were frequently seen in the John Crow Mountains; whether specimens of this species can still be found there nowadays is not known. Porter suspects that they no longer occur in the southern and eastern parts of the island. On Jamaica, in addition to the Black-billed Amazon, there is also the Yellow-billed Amazon (*Amazona collaria*). The latter prefers higher-lying areas, but nevertheless the two species sometimes flock in mixed parties (G). The Black-billed Amazon eats the spicy grains of pimento trees (F).

Breeding: In 1979, Noegel in Florida reported a successful breeding in which one young was raised (L). The average number of eggs is four. In 1973 in London, a Black-billed was crossed with a White-fronted Amazon (*Amazona albifrons*). From two eggs laid, one chick hatched after twenty-five days, but died two days later.

Remarks: Black-billed Amazons are extremely rare today. In captivity they become tame and get along well with others; the females have shown themselves to be more given to biting than the males (G, L). Russ speaks of *Amazona agilis* as a real "*krik*," a very shrill shrieker.

PUERTO RICAN AMAZON

5.1 *Amazona vittata vittata*
‡ (Boddaert) 1783

Range: The island of Puerto Rico; formerly also the island of Vieques

Description:
Length: 29–30 cm.
Basic color: Dark green; underside lighter, yellowish

Forehead: Red band
Crown, occiput, nape: Black-edged feathers
Lores: Red
Eye area, cheeks, throat: Black-edged feathers
Abdomen: Sometimes dull light red
Primaries: Dark blue
Primary coverts: Outer ones dark blue
Secondaries: Outer feathers with blue outer vanes and narrow dull green edges
Underside of flight feathers: Blue-green
Tail: Green with narrow yellow-green tips; bases of lateral feathers have red on inner vanes; outermost tail feathers blue edged
Under tail coverts: Yellow-green
Beak: Yellowish horn-colored (F); light gray (P)
Cere: Brownish (G)
Eye ring: White
Iris: Brown (F); red (G); yellow (L)
Legs: Yellow-brown

Sex-related differences: None

Young: Little or no red on the forehead (G); no different from adults (F, L)

Life in the wild: Its habitat today is probably limited to the Luquillo National Forest; in this wilderness, there are at best only dispersed representatives of this species, threatened by extinction. While in 1864 the Puerto Rican Amazon was still common, already in 1912 it was seldom observed, and since then the stock has decreased even further. A count taken between 1953 and 1956 in the Luquillo National Forest Reserve in the eastern part of the island, the stronghold of this species, showed that the largest flock seen consisted of 200 animals; it was concluded from observation that these constituted most of the remaining Puerto Rican Amazons. By 1965, their number shrank to probably around fifty specimens, which caused Dr. C. Kepler to start a project for the preservation of the species (1968–70). His work was continued in 1972 by Dr. N. Snyder (F).

The reasons for this decimation are basically the clearing of the forests, hunting by the natives, and hurricanes, but animal enemies also contributed considerably. Different species of hawks (*Buteo jamaicensis, Buteo platypterus, Accipiter striatus*), rats, and also prowling cats go out and rob eggs and nestlings—they even attack fully grown birds. Furthermore, the Puerto Rican Amazon is in competition with the Pearly-eyed Thrasher (*Margarops fuscatus*). This aggressive bird competes for food and nesting sites, and robs eggs and nestlings. For years it has spread at the expense of the amazons. Since 1973 several attempts have been made to restrict the Pearly-eyed Thrasher. It was discovered that it prefers nesting cavities with little depth, while the amazons like to breed in deeper tree cavities. In 1976, when special nesting sites were readied for both, the thrasher left the deep cavities for the amazons; thus the threat from this quarter probably may be considered a thing of the past (F).

Breeding: The breeding success of free-living Puerto Rican Amazons has risen from 11–26% to the present 71%, so that there is hope that this species may be preserved after all. However, H. Müller, after his travels to the island in the summer of 1981, reported only nineteen living specimens. Breeding attempts with captured animals until now have been unsuccessful; all eggs laid have been infertile.

5.1 *vittata vittata*

117

Above: Puerto Rican Amazon (*A. vittata vittata*): female at her nest.
Left: Puerto Rican Amazon nestlings at the Institute of Tropical Forestry field station in Puerto Rico.

**Puerto Rican Amazon (*A. vittata vittata*): adult
eating native fruit.**

The breeding grounds in Puerto Rico are found at 700 m. above sea level on the western side of the mountains in the Luquillo National Forest; formerly, the parrots also nested in the northwestern part of the island in rock cavities. All breeding cavities found recently (with one exception) have been in colorado trees (*Cyrilla racemiflora*), 6–15 m. above the ground (F). The breeding season lies between the end of February and the beginning of June; i.e., during the dry season, when the palm trees bear fruit. On the average, three eggs are laid, incubated for about twenty-six days, and the nestling period lasts for about another nine weeks.

Remarks: As Rodriquez-Vidal noted, the Puerto Rican Amazons eat the fruits of more than fifty different plants; since then, his list has been enlarged by even more species (F). The main staples are the palm tree *Prestoea montana* in the spring and the plant *Dacryodes excelsa* in the fall.

5.2 *Amazona vittata gracilipes*
† Ridgway

5.2 *vittata gracilipes*

Range: formerly on the island of Culebra, east of Puerto Rico

Description: (See Forshaw)
Length: Smaller than nominate form
Legs: Smaller and narrower feet

Note: Still generally known in 1899, this subspecies of the Puerto Rican Amazon has been extinct since 1912. Only three specimens are known to science, one of which can be seen in the National Museum in Washington, D.C. (F).

WHITE-FRONTED AMAZON

6.1 *Amazona albifrons albifrons* (Sparrmann) 1788

Range: Mexico, from Nayarit in the midwest to Chiapas in the south; southwestern Guatemala
Description:
Length: 26 cm.
Basic color: Green, covering feathers edged with black
Forehead: White
Crown: White in front, sometimes yellowish; in the back, dull blue edged with black
Occiput: Dull blue edged with black
Eye area: Red
Breast: Dark feather edges
Primaries: Outer vanes green, blue toward the tips
Secondaries: Blue outer vanes
Underside of flight feathers: Blue-green
Tail: Green with yellow tips, lateral feathers red at bases
Tail coverts: Yellow-green
Beak: Light yellow
Cere: Light
Eye ring: White
Iris: Pale yellow
Legs: Light gray (F); brown-gray (G)

Sex-related differences: Obvious. *Male:* Alula and primary coverts are red; more red to the rear of the eyes; secondaries and outer vanes of the primaries are a more intense blue (Müller, in *Die Voliere*, 1978/1). *Female:* No red in the wings; iris red-brown

Young: No red in the wings; yellow feathers at the edge of the forehead; iris almost black, then muddy yellow (G). On the head more blue than white (Bedford). On the head, only lores red; white feathers of forehead have a yellowish tinge (F).

Life in the wild: According to Forshaw, the birds preferably inhabit dry woods and bushlands to an altitude of 1850 m. They live in giant cactus thickets, thorn bushes, and evergreen forests, and also occur in rain forests of moderate elevation. They are not found in the high rain forests or in the damp areas of the Caribbean flatlands. In part, the flocks will move about; in spring and summer they visit the western part of El Salvador and the dry, low-lying tropical zone in eastern Guatemala, though they do not occur there during the dry winter months. In addition to the usual items, figs, leaf buds, and cactus fruit are part of their diet. Forshaw and Low emphasize the flight pattern of the White-fronted Amazon. It attracts attention by incessantly changing the direction of flight, a vacillating which seems almost aratingalike. These birds are said not to be shy in the wild; Forshaw reports that they do not fly away if someone is under the tree.

Breeding: The first breeding took place in 1922 in Japan. In 1934, a cross with a Green-cheeked Amazon (*Amazona viridigenalis*) succeeded. In the U.S.A., the first breeding was announced in 1948. Since then, the number of the White-fronted Amazons in Europe has increased repeatedly. The first breeding in Germany was recorded by H. Müller. He reports a two-week-long, noisy courtship. He noticed that during incubation the female evacuated her droppings only about every three days. From three eggs, one youngster hatched. The White-fronted Amazon lays two to four eggs; the incubation period lasts twenty-eight to thirty days; the nestling period is sixty to sixty-five days. In 1973 in London, a cross with a Black-billed Amazon (*Amazona agilis*) was successful. Crossing with a Blue-fronted Amazon (*Amazona aestiva*) is also known.

Remarks: There are conflicting reports about the behavior of this amazon in captivity. Pinter talks about a good talent for talking and a decrease of screeching during the course of adaptation. Bedford recommends keeping White-fronted Amazons in aviaries, because they are unfriendly and likely to bite. De Grahl, on the other hand, describes them as quiet, friendly animals which become tame after initial timidity; they are, however, able to mimic only noises.

6.1 *albifrons albifrons*

6.2 *Amazona albifrons saltuensis* Nelson

Range: Mexico, in the area south of the Sonora river and around Sinaloa (northwestern Durango)

Yellow-lored Amazon (*A. xantholora*): female above, male below.

Hispaniolan Amazon (*A. ventralis*).

6.2 albifrons saltuensis

Range: From south Mexico in the extreme southeast of Veracruz and in the northeastern part of Chiapas, through Guatemala, Belize, El Salvador, Honduras, and Nicaragua, to northwestern Costa Rica

Description: Smaller than the nominate form

Life in the wild: The birds prefer dry, steppelike areas with single trees or groups of trees and dry tropical shrubs. Sometimes, they are seen with Yellow-lored Amazons (*Amazona xantholora*). Slud has described the aratingalike, swerving pattern of flight (L).

Description:
Length: 27 cm.
Nape: The blue on the head extends backward
Sides of neck and back: Feathers strongly tinged with blue

6.3 *Amazona albifrons nana* W. de W. Miller

6.3 albifrons nana

YELLOW-LORED AMAZON

---

7. *Amazona xantholora* (Gray) 1859

Range: Extreme southeastern Mexico, in the eastern and central part of the Yucatán Peninsula; the island of Cozumel; Belize; the island of Roatán

Description:
Length: 26 cm.
Basic color: Green, blackish edge to feathers
Forehead: White
Crown: White
Occiput: Dull blue, edged with black
Lores: Yellow
Eye area: Red
Ear coverts: Black
Cheeks: Upper part red
Primaries: Green, shading into blue-purple toward the tips
Primary coverts: Red
Secondaries: Blue-purple
Underside of flight feathers: Blue-green
Under wing coverts: Blue-green
Tail: Green with yellow tips, lateral feathers red at bases
Tail coverts: Yellow-green

7 xantholora

Breeding: The world's first breeding took place for A. Maier in Switzerland in 1980. The animals are ready to breed from March to July. A clutch will consist of up to five eggs; the incubation period lasts for twenty-six days; the young leave the nest after about six weeks.

HISPANIOLAN AMAZON

8. *Amazona ventralis*
   (P. L. S. Müller) 1776

Range: The island of Hispaniola (Haiti and the Dominican Republic) and nearby small islands (Gonâve, Saona); Puerto Rico

Description:
Length: 28–29 cm.
Basic color: Green
Forehead: White
Crown: Dull blue, black edged
Occiput, nape: Black-edged feathers
Lores: White
Ear coverts: Dark brown
Cheeks: Upper part dull blue edged with black
Chin: Reddish spot (F)

Beak: Yellowish horn-colored
Cere: Light gray
Eye ring: White
Iris: Reddish (G, P); yellowish brown (F)
Legs: Brownish yellow (G); pale gray (F)

Sex-related differences: *Male:* Red wing speculum (L). *Female:* Red only beneath the eyes and on the upper part of the cheeks; little or no red in the wings; ear coverts paler; forehead and crown dull blue instead of white, sometimes with single white feathers

Young: Like females, but the upper part of the cheeks green, interspersed with red; lores yellow with occasional green feathers mixed in; primary coverts still green or only a little red

Life in the wild: The Yellow-lored Amazon is sometimes confused with the White-fronted Amazon (*Amazona albifrons*). Some authors, like Bedford and Low, list them as a single species. Indeed, they repeatedly form common flocks, but the habitat of the Yellow-lored Amazon is more limited, and it prefers more dense forest. According to Griscom (F), these amazons cover large distances; they fly from the Yucatán Peninsula to spend the day on the island of Cozumel, 15 km. distant.

8 ventralis

Hispaniolan Amazon (*A. ventralis*).

Cuban Amazon (*A. leucocephala leucocephala*).

Breast: Black-edged feathers
Abdomen: Center wine-red (G); lower abdomen brown-red, variable (F, P)
Thighs: Bluish (L)
Primaries: Blue, tips darker
Primary coverts: Blue, tips darker
Secondaries: Blue, outer vanes narrowly edged with green
Secondary coverts: Blue, outer vanes narrowly edged with green
Underside of flight feathers: Blue-green
Tail: Green with yellow tips, lateral feathers red at bases, outermost feathers tinged with blue (F); lateral feathers with blue outer vanes, yellow inner vanes, and red bases (L)
Tail coverts: Yellow-green
Beak: Yellowish horn-colored
Cere: White
Eye ring: White
Iris: Dark brown (F, P); yellowish to reddish (G)
Legs: Reddish gray

Sex-related differences: None

Young: More white on the forehead, with yellowish shimmer but no blue; lower abdomen slightly orange-red (G)

Life in the wild: These parrots inhabit the high montane forests as well as the settled lowlands; they always appear opportunistically where food can be found. In the dry flatlands, they eat the fruit of cactus and guayacan trees. In humid areas they feed, among other things, on guava, plantain, banana, and invade fields of corn and peas. Palm seeds, nuts, and blossoms are also on the menu.

Breeding: Formerly, the Hispaniolan Amazon was thought to be the female of the Cuban Amazon (*Amazona leucocephala*). At the onset of the breeding season in late March and early April, the males repeat a kind of regular, melodic babbling. A nest has been found even in a cactus (F). The female lays two to four eggs and incubates them for about twenty-five days; the nestling period lasts sixty to sixty-five days. Captive breeding first succeeded in 1971 in the zoo of Jersey. In his book, de Grahl repeats Gates's information about this event: During incubation, the male fed the female regularly. After the single youngster hatched, the mother continued to sit firmly on the nest for another ten days; after sixty-one days, the youngster left the box. The male helped with the feeding of the nestling. After thirteen weeks, the young Hispaniolan Amazon was able to eat by itself.

Remarks: Several amazon keepers report that rose hips are well liked, and the larvae of mealybugs are also in demand (Murray, in Low).

CUBAN AMAZON

9.1 *Amazona leucocephala leucocephala* (Linné) 1758

Range: Eastern and central Cuba

Description:
Length: 32 cm.
Basic color: Green, all covering feathers on head, back, and abdomen edged with black, with the exception of the reddish throat feathers
Forehead: White
Crown: White
Occiput: Blue (L)
Nape: Blue (L)
Lores: Pink
Eye region: Narrow white strip all the way around
Ear coverts: Dull black
Cheeks: Pink
Throat and some breast feathers: Pink
Abdomen: Variably wine-red, edged with dark green
Carpal edge: Blue
Primaries: Blue outer vanes, black inner vanes
Primary coverts: Blue
Secondaries: Dull blue, outer vanes narrowly edged with green

Underside of flight feathers: Blue green
Tail: Upper side green with yellow-green tips, underside yellow-green; lateral feathers red at bases (F), also yellow and orange (L); extreme outer feathers edged with blue
Tail coverts: Yellow-green, upper feathers lightly edged with black
Beak: White to horn-colored
Cere: White (P); light gray (G)
Eye ring: White
Iris: Red-brown (G); dark brown (P); pale olive green (F)
Legs: Red-brown to pink (P, F); yellow-brown (G)

Sex-related differences: None

Young: Cheek spot merely indicated, feathers barely edged black; less pink, particularly on abdomen

Life in the wild: According to de Grahl, fifty years ago there were still large flocks near the town of Cotorro. Extensive clearing, cultivation, and hunting have caused the Cuban Amazon to retreat to the interior of the island, into the mangrove-covered lowlands and the mountains. They live in isolated areas and, particularly while eating, permit humans to approach (F). Palm seeds, soft shoots of pines,

leaf buds, grapefruit, and the inner parts of blossoms constitute their diet.

Breeding: Between March and the end of June, three to four eggs are laid and incubated for thirty days; the young leave the nest after sixty-five to seventy days. The first successful breeding occurred in Japan. In 1956, the Keston Bird Farm in England was successful: the animals had absolute peace, and during breeding they were fed cooked fish. In 1960 there were offspring in the U.S., and in 1974 in East Germany.

According to *Die Gefiederte Welt*, a crossing with a Blue-fronted Amazon (*Amazona aestiva*) took place in Holland in 1885. Bedford reports that a female Cuban Amazon paired with a male Adelaide Rosella (*Platycercus adelaidae*), but the amazon died before the somewhat too optimistically hoped-for breeding occurred.

Remarks: Boosey and V. McDaniels came independently to the conviction that these amazons would rather fly than climb (L). In the zoo in Prague it was noted that the Cuban Amazons like extraordinarily much to bathe (G). Pinter describes them as very tame and affectionate. De Grahl speaks of birds initially shy when caught in the wild which may develop into good or bad talkers, and attests to their playfulness and vivacity. Low, with Bedford, is of the opinion that they are average talkers which, because of their noisiness, had better be kept in aviaries or bird rooms.

9.1 *leucocephala leucocephala*

9.2 *Amazona leucocephala*
‡ *palmarum* Todd 1916

Range: Western Cuba and the Isle of Pines

Description:
Basic color: Darker green
Throat: Stronger red
Abdomen: Stronger red (purplish) larger area

Above: Cuban Amazon (*A. leucocephala caymanensis*).
Below: Hispaniolan Amazon (*A. ventralis*).

Von einer absonderlichen Arth Papageyen.

Psittacus Leococephalus.

Dieser Vogel ist einer Spannen und Fingers lang/und hat einen Schnabel so 2. Finger breit/und gantz weiß ist/desgleichen siehet er auch oben auff dem Kopff weiß. Sein mittler Augapffel ist gantz schwartz/der Nebenschein aber ist Eisenfarb: oben auff dem Kopff alwo er weiß ist/werden etliche schwartze Strichlein durchmischet. Am Hintertheil des Kopffs/an dem Halß/Rücken/Flügeln/und auff dem Bürtzel siehet er gantz dunckelgrün/unten an dem Halß aber und zu eusserst seiner Flügel/pralet eine hoch Cinnoberrothe Farb hervor/welche dem Vogel nicht wenig Zieraht giebet/auff der Brust und Hüfften/siehet er gleichfals grün/zwischen den Obertheil der Bein und der Brust/siehet er braunroth/an den Flügeln hat er etlich blawe mit weiß vermischte Federn/welche seine Schwingfedern bedecken/hinten an dem Bauch siehet er gelb/der Schwantz ist in der Mitten roth/auff den Seitē aber roth mit gelb und blau gleichsam vermischet. Alle Federn sind an den Spitzen schwartz/am übrigen Theil grün. Die Füß und Bein sehen aschenfarb/daß deßwegen wohl dieser Vogel wegen unterschiedlich ᴄᴂ und mancherley Farben τ‹ικιλὸϛ versicolor könte genennet werden/dieweil er über sieben Farben hat/worunter doch die grüne die vornehmste ist.

Above: Cuban Amazon (*A. leucocephala*)

Left: Excerpt from the *Vogelbuch* of Conrad Gesner. Facsimile reprint of the German-language edition of 1669, Schlütersche Verlagsanstalt Hannover.

About a Singular Kind of Parrot
Psittacus Leucocephalus.

This bird is a span and a finger long and has a beak about two fingers wide, which is all white and looks just as white as the top of its head. The middle of its eyeball is all black; its appearance, however, is iron colored. On top of its head where it is white, several black lines are mixed in. On the back of the head, on the neck, wings, and rump, it appears completely dark green. Underneath its neck and at the ends of its wings shines a bright vermilion color which gives the bird no mean adornment. On the breast and haunches it is also green. Between the upper part of the leg and the breast it looks brown-red. On the wings it has several feathers blue mixed with white, which cover its flight feathers. Behind the abdomen there is yellow. The tail is red in the middle, but the sides are red equally mixed with yellow and blue. All feathers are black at the tips, with the rest green. The feet and legs are ash colored, so that this bird, because of the varied and different colors, could be called *poikilos, versicolor*, since it has more than seven colors, of which green is predominant.

9.2 *leucocephala palmarum*

Range: Grand Cayman Island

Description:
Length: Minimally larger than nominate form, 32–33 cm.
Basic color: Rather yellow-green, feather edging paler
Forehead: Less extensive white; mixed with red or yellowish tinged (L)
Eye region: No white behind the eyes
Cheeks: A green stripe separates the red of the cheeks from that of the neck
Abdomen: A rather small red area
Eye ring: Gray (L)

Life in the wild: They live exclusively in mangrove forests (L).

Breeding: The world's first breeding succeeded in 1974 for Noegel in Florida.

Remarks: These birds are described as extremely temperature-sensitive.

Breeding: Since 1975, Noegel in Florida has achieved repeated breeding successes with this subspecies (L).

9.3 *Amazona leucocephala* ‡ *caymanensis* (Cory)

9.3 *leucocephala caymanensis*

9.4 *Amazona leucocephala* ‡ *hesterna* Bangs 1916

Range: The islands of Little Cayman and Cayman Brac

Description: Narrower head
Length: Smaller than nominate form
Basic color: Rather yellow-green, feather edging stronger black
Crown: No white
Lores: Barely red
Cheeks and throat: Stronger pink (F)
Abdomen: Red area more strongly colored (purplish) and extending farther up toward the breast
Eye ring: Bluish

9.4 *leucocephala hesterna*

Description:
Length: Somewhat longer than nominate form; 34 cm. (L)
Crown: More extensive and backward extending white
Lores and eye region: White also beneath the eyes, toward the lores, and on the upper cheeks
Abdomen: Red area is smaller or nonexistent
Tail: Lateral feathers barely red at bases, the two outermost ones with red areas and blue edges

Sex-related differences: *Female:* The white on the forehead is less widespread than on the male; on the lores, the red is completely missing (L).

Life in the wild: Johnston reported in 1971 that Cuban Amazons were seen frequently on both islands (F). Noegel, during his stay in 1974–75, could not discover any amazons on Little Cayman. Forshaw speculates that the animals formerly sighted there had flown across from the island of Cayman Brac, 11 km. distant. There exists, according to Noegel, a flock of thirty to forty birds which remains predominantly in the heavily overgrown region toward the steep eastern coast, but roams through the entire island on a regular route in their search for food. Papaya fruits are eaten with pleasure.

Life in the wild: According to King (1976), the Bahamas Amazons were able to stabilize their numbers again. On Abaco, there are about 300 specimens; those living on Great Inagua are estimated at 500 (F).

Breeding: All the nests discovered on Abaco were in limestone cavities with a depth between 1.7 and 2.5 m. No successful breeding in captivity is known; in 1909, from three eggs one young hatched, but died.

9.5 *Amazona leucocephala* ‡ *bahamensis* (Bryant)

Range: The Bahamas: Great Inagua, Abaco, perhaps Acklins Island; formerly on Long Island, Crooked Island, and Fortune Island

9.5 *leucocephala bahamensis*

Above: Yellow-billed Amazon *(A. collaria)*: adult pair.
Left: Yellow-billed Amazon *(A. collaria)*: adult.

Yellow-billed Amazon (*A. collaria*).

YELLOW-BILLED AMAZON

10. *Amazona collaria* (Linné) 1758

Range: Jamaica

Description:
Length: 28–29 cm.
Basic color: Green, yellowish pale green on the underside
Forehead: Narrow white
Crown: Bluish, feather edging black
Occiput, nape: Black edging
Lores: Dull bluish
Eye region: Blue, narrowly white behind eyes
Ear coverts: Dull gray-blue with green shimmer
Cheeks: Wine-red (lower part)
Chin: Wine-red
Throat and sides of neck: Wine-red, most feathers edged slightly green or dull blue
Thighs: At bottom, pale light blue
Primaries: Blue outer vanes, black inner vanes
Primary coverts: Blue (outer)
Secondaries: Outer vanes dull blue edged with green
Underside of flight feathers: Blue-green
Back and rump: Pale green

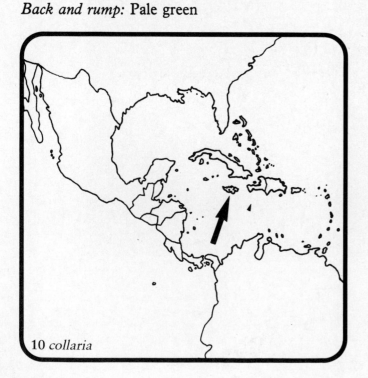

10 *collaria*

Tail: Green with yellow tips; lateral feathers red at bases (F), pink and yellow (L); outer vanes red (P); outermost feathers narrowly edged with blue
Upper tail coverts: Bright yellow-green
Beak: Light horn-yellow
Cere: Horn-colored
Eye ring: White (to gray)
Iris: Black-brown
Legs: Brown-gray (G); pale pink (F)

Sex-related differences: *Male:* According to Porter, some bright orange feathers at alula (not certain – L)

Young: No differences known

Life in the wild: They live in the John Crow Mountains, on Mount Diablo and in the "Cockpit Country," inhabiting forested mountain regions, preferably linden forests in areas of moderate humidity. From the John Crow Mountains they undertake daily excursions to the eastern side of the Blue Mountains in order to eat. Pisang fruits are eaten with pleasure. Occasionally, these amazons damage fields and plantations; they can be found in cultivated wooded areas, but do not breed there. They sometimes form mixed flocks with the less common Black-billed Amazon (*Amazona agilis*) (F).

Breeding: Up to four eggs are laid. The only known pure breeding took place in the United States in 1970, but Low gives no further comments. On the Keston Farm in England, crossbreeding with a male Festive Amazon (*Amazona festiva*) took place; the three young animals resembled their father (G).

Remarks: Having become cautious because of persecution, Yellow-billed Amazons in the wild will not tolerate close approach. In captivity, however, they become very affectionate and are lovable, as de Grahl is able to report; he does indicate, however, that they have only limited talking talent. Bedford also mentions the noisiness of these birds.

YELLOW-FACED AMAZON

11. *Amazona xanthops* (Spix) 1824

Range: Eastern and central Brazil, from the south of Piauí through Goiás to Mato Grosso, southward to the vicinity of São Paulo

Description:
Length: 27–28 cm.
Basic color: Yellowish green
Forehead: Yellow
Crown: Yellow
Occiput: Yellow
Nape: Dark green edging and blackish tips
Lores, ear coverts: Orange-yellow
Breast, abdomen: Upper part green with wide dark green feather edging, interspersed with yellow feathers in older animals; lower part of breast and abdomen yellow, orange toward the sides; lower abdomen green with dark edging
Thighs: Light green with dark edging
Carpal edge: Pale yellow-green
Primaries: Dark green with narrow greenish yellow edging
Primary coverts: Green with dull blue edging
Secondaries: Green, narrowly edged with yellow-green
Underside of flight feathers: Blue-green
Back: Dark green
Tail: Central feathers green; lateral, yellow-green with orange-red band at bases
Tail coverts: Yellow-green
Beak: Horn-colored; upper mandible grey at tip (F, P, L); upper part of upper mandible darker, tip white (G).
Cere: light; pink (G)
Eye ring: White
Iris: Yellow
Legs: Pale gray (F); dark gray (P)

Sex-related differences: None

Young: Less yellow on head, only at crown, eye region, ear coverts, and cheeks; green head feathers with dark blue-green edges and blackish tips; underside of body completely green, feathers edged with dark-green; brown iris (F)

Life in the wild: The Yellow-faced Amazon is a typical inhabitant of the low bushlands of the plateaus in the interior of eastern Brazil, according to Sick. Half-ripe guavas are an addition to the usual diet worth mentioning.

Breeding: Nothing known

Remarks: To this amazon little talent for mimicry or cunning has been ascribed (G); Low describes it as outstandingly quiet, but by no means timid.

11 *xanthops*

LILAC-CROWNED AMAZON

12.1 *Amazona finschi finschi* (Sclater) 1864

Range: Central and southwest Mexico, south of Sinaloa and Durango, along the Pacific Ocean southward to Oaxaca

137

Yellow-faced Amazon (*A. xanthops*). Coloration varies from animal to animal; here the rose-red cere is striking.

**Lilac-crowned Amazon (*A. finschi finschi*). The
feathers of one wing have been heavily clipped.**

Description: Smaller than the Green-cheeked Amazon (*Amazona viridigenalis*) (L)
Length: 33 cm.
Basic color: Green; underside paler, yellowish green; black feather edging on back, breast, and abdomen
Forehead: Red to red-brown
Crown: Red-brown
Occiput: Violet
Nape: Violet towards the sides
Lores: Red-brown
Cheeks: Yellow-green, without edging
Ear coverts: Yellow-green, without edging
Primaries: Blue-violet, green toward the base
Secondaries: Green, turning blue toward the tips
Wing speculum: On the five forward primaries: red outer vanes (G); inner vanes red at base (F)
Tail: Green with yellow-green tips, outer vanes of outermost feathers blue-edged toward the bases (F)
Beak: Light gray (P); horn-colored (F), yellowish with darker tip (G)
Cere: Light gray (P); dark gray (G)
Eye ring: Light gray (P); dark gray (G)
Iris: Orange-red
Legs: Green-gray (F, P); blue-gray (G)

Sex-related differences: *Female:* Smaller

12.1 *finschi finschi*

Young: Dark-brown iris, later ochre, then orange (G)

Life in the wild: The habitat of the Lilac-crowned Amazons extends from sea level up to 2200 m. They are found on wooded mountain slopes (Sierra Madre), as well as in the hilly flatlands. They have been observed in forests of pine and oak and also occur in arid tropical areas. In addition to the usual items, figs, buds, and blossoms in the treetops are eaten (F). C.W. Beebe describes these parrots as skilled flyers which often end their wave-shaped flight with a wide, curving arc to the earth.

Breeding: Courtship and egg laying take place between February and May. Up to four eggs are laid; the young hatch after twenty-six to twenty-eight days, but remain another eight to nine weeks in the nest. The initial breeding success happened in the U.S.A. for Mercer in 1949. Other breedings in the U.S.A. have been recorded. De Grahl describes the development of nestlings whose parents were only three to four years old when they bred successfully at the San Diego Zoo. The young had to be raised by hand since the parents stopped feeding them after five days, probably because of a lack of needed quiet. Eleven days after hatching the young opened their eyes for the first time; two days later, the first signs of growing feathers could be seen; after another four days the unopened feather sheaths were visible. The animals left the nest cavity at about eight weeks of age, but required another two months to become completely self-sufficient. Low mentions a 1972 crossbreeding with a male Blue-cheeked Amazon (*Amazona dufresniana rhodocorytha*) in Tampa, Florida.

Remarks: In human hands, these birds become trusting and learn to imitate various sounds, but because of their high-pitched voices, there is little possibility for variation. De Grahl awarded them the attributes of good nature and playfulness.

12.2 *Amazona finschi woodi* Moore

Range: Northwestern Mexico; from the extreme southeast of Sonora and southwest of Chihuahua southward to Sinaloa and Durango

12.2 *finschi woodi*

Description:
Length: Larger than nominate form (G)
Basic color: The green is less yellowish
Forehead and crown: Red-brown stripe is narrower, duller

GREEN-CHEEKED AMAZON

13. *Amazona viridigenalis* (Cassin) 1853

Range: Northeastern Mexico; from Nuevo Leon and Tamaulipas through San Luis Potosí into the north of Veracruz

Description:
Length: 33 cm.

Basic color: Green; underside paler and yellowish, blackish feather edges
Forehead: Red, feathers yellow at base
Crown: Red, yellow at base
Nape: Strongly black edged
Lores: Red, yellow at base
Eye region: Violet band from above the eyes to the sides of the neck
Cheeks and ear region: Bright green, feathers not edged
Breast: Feathers of the upper part have black tips (L)
Primaries: Outer vanes blue-violet, green toward the bases
Secondaries: Green, blue toward the tips
Wing speculum: First five primaries red at the bases of outer vanes
Tail: Green with wide yellow-green tips
Beak: Yellowish horn-colored
Cere: Light
Eye ring: White (P); gray (G)
Iris: Yellow
Legs: Pale gray-green (P, F); gray-brown (G)

Sex-related differences: *Female:* Less red on head (G)

Young: Red only on forehead, crown green; blue stripe on side of neck is missing (G)

13 *viridigenalis*

Above: Lilac-crowned Amazon (A. finschi woodi).
Left, above: Young Green-cheeked Amazon (A. viridigenalis).
Left, below: Adult Green-cheeked Amazon (A. viridigenalis). Its tail has been damaged on cage wires.

Green-cheeked Amazon (*A. viridigenalis*).

Life in the wild: They live in the forest areas along riverbeds at the edges of dense forest, in damp lowlands where fields give way to single tracts of forest, on dry open mountain ridges which are overgrown with pine and oak, as well as in the tropical forests of canyons. In Mexico, the Red-lored Amazon (*Amazona autumnalis*) and Yellow-crowned Amazon (*Amazona ochrocephala*) are more strongly represented than the Green-cheeked Amazon.

Breeding: From the end of March through April, two or three eggs are laid. The first captive breeding happened in 1970 in the Los Angeles Zoo. Between 1972 and 1977, Springman in Texas obtained from one pair eighteen young, of which one young pair bred in 1976 (L). Crossbreeding has occurred with a Blue-fronted Amazon (*Amazona aestiva*), according to Wolters; and in England in 1934 with a White-fronted Amazon (*Amazona albifrons*), according to de Grahl. Low reports a pair of lutinos, which were kept by a bird fancier in the U.S.A.

Remarks: The Green-cheeked Amazon shows only a moderate mimetic talent in captivity and is said to be quite loud (G).

RED-LORED AMAZON

14.1 *Amazona autumnalis autumnalis* (Linné) 1758

Range: Mexico, on the eastern (Caribbean) slope, from Tamaulipas southward; eastern Guatemala, Belize, Honduras to the northern border of Nicaragua, and on the Bay Islands (Roatán, Barbareta)

Description:
Length: 34–35 cm.
Basic color: Green
Forehead: Red

14.1 *autumnalis autumnalis*

Crown, occiput, and nape: Lilac-blue (P); green with lilac-blue tips (F); blackish feather edges
Lores: Red
Cheeks: Upper part yellow, feathers red at bases
Throat: Yellow-green
Carpal edge: Yellowish light-green
Primaries: Green, dark blue toward the tips
Secondaries: Green, with tips shading to blue
Wing speculum: First five primaries red at bases
Tail: Green central feathers; lateral feathers with wide yellow-green tips; outer vanes of the outermost feathers blue edged (F)
Beak: Tip of the lower mandible gray horn-colored, upper mandible light horn-colored; white-gray (P)
Cere: Light
Eye ring: White
Iris: Dark brown (P); orange (F, G) (see Sex-related differences)
Legs: Light gray (P); greenish gray (F); dark gray (G)

Sex-related differences: *Male:* Iris golden (L). *Female:* Iris dark brown (L)

Young: Less red on forehead and lores; upper part of cheeks and ear coverts interspersed with green; iris dark brown; beak darker (G); neck feathers without purple tips (L); young the same as adults (Vane, in Low)

Life in the wild: Red-lored Amazons are among the few species of amazons which do not live in dry areas, but prefer humid tropical forest regions and breed in the rain forest. They are also found in pine forests along riverbeds, in the vicinity of mangrove swamps, and in cultivated forests. Their habitat extends from sea level to 1100 m. in the interior. The fruits of various kinds of palm trees, half-ripe mangoes and citrus fruits enrich their menu (F). They have been observed in the company of macaws. They are characterized as shy and watchful.

Breeding: The breeding season is from February to June; the clutch contains three or four eggs, from which the young hatch after twenty-five to twenty-six days, then remain in the nest for another seventy days. A breeding occurred in England in 1957; the report by E. N. T. Vane is repeated by Low, Wolters, and de Grahl. Of three eggs, only one was fertile; a Grey Parrot was used as a foster mother. During incubation she was fed a mixture of seeds, dark bread soaked in milk, sprouts, and different kinds of vegetables. She helped the chick hatch by biting open the tip of the egg and remained firmly sitting on the nest for two weeks after the hatching. The nestling was given its first meal on the second day, after which the foster mother fed it every two to three hours with crop milk. After six weeks, the intervals between feedings became shorter, the rations smaller, and the nourishment of thicker texture. From the tenth day on, the young amazon had its eyes open; after eight weeks, it left the nest and climbed around on the climbing tree. Besides this, only a crossbreeding with a Blue-fronted Amazon (*Amazona aestiva*) is mentioned in the literature.

Remarks: Vane (G) and Pinter remark that it takes a long time for Red-lored Amazons to become tame with humans. Pinter considers them poor talkers that shriek loudly when they are startled; Vane, on the other hand, certifies good talking ability.

14.2 *Amazona autumnalis salvini* (Salvadori) 1891

Range: Eastern Nicaragua; eastern and southwestern Costa Rica; Panama, the island of Coiba, and other small islands of the Canal Zone; western Colombia and the extreme northwest of Venezuela

Description:
Cheeks: Bright green
Ear coverts: Bright green
Chin: Sometimes wine-red
Tail: Lateral feathers have red inner vanes at the bases

Life in the wild: In northeastern Nicaragua, their range overlaps that of *autumnalis autumnalis* and in the extreme southwest of Colombia that of *autumnalis lilacina*. This subspecies has repeatedly been sighted with the Mealy Amazon (*Amazona farinosa*) in Costa Rica.

Breeding: In 1973, a female was crossbred with a male Blue-fronted Amazon (*Amazona aestiva xanthopteryx*) (L).

Remarks: Low describes it as a noisy bird.

14.2 *autumnalis salvini*

Above: Red-lored Amazon *(A. autumnalis autumnalis)*
Left, above: Red-lored Amazon *(A. autumnalis salvini)*.
Left, below: Red-lored Amazon *(A. autumnalis lilacina)*.

Red-lored Amazon (*A. autumnalis diadema*).

14.3 *Amazona autumnalis lilacina* Lesson

Range: Western Ecuador, north of the Gulf of Guayaquil

Description: Similar to *Amazona autumnalis salvini*
Length: Measurements vary between 32 and 35 cm.
Forehead: Red extends in a line beyond the eye
Crown: Green with lilac tips, reddish violet edges
Lores: Dark red
Cheeks: Yellowish green
Tail: Inner vanes red at bases
Beak: Black (G)

Life in the wild: This amazon lives in the tropical zone in the hot equatorial region.

Breeding: In 1946, Putnam in the U.S. achieved a breeding.

Remarks: Low writes that this amazon does become tame.

14.3 *autumnalis lilacina*

14.4 *Amazona autumnalis diadema* (Spix) 1824

Range: Northwestern Brazil between the Rio Negro and the upper Amazon

14.4 *autumnalis diadema*

Description:
Length: 36 cm. (larger than the nominate form)
Crown: Lilac, bluish in front, green in the center
Occiput, nape: Green with greenish-yellow edging
Neck: Lower part green with lilac
Lores: Crimson (dark)
Cheeks: Yellowish green
Chin: Often wine-red (G)
Cere: Light, with small red bristles

Sex-related differences: *Male:* Tail feathers are 2 cm. shorter than in the female (G)

Young: Little red and blue

Life in the wild: This amazon lives near the equator in high temperatures and humidity.

Remarks: According to de Grahl, in captivity it learns to imitate sounds well.

RED-TAILED AMAZON

15. *Amazona brasiliensis* (Linné) 1758

Range: Southeastern Brazil from southeast of São Paulo to Rio Grande do Sul

Description:
Length: 36–37 cm.
Basic color: Green; underside paler; yellow-edged wing coverts
Forehead: Dull red
Crown: Pink, mauve edges, yellow at the bases; weakly orange (G)
Nape: Pink, base yellow, pale edges; weakly orange (G)
Lores: Dull red
Ear coverts: Dull reddish-blue
Cheeks, neck, and chin: Dull reddish blue, mauve edges (F)
Sides of head and chin: Turquoise (G)
Carpal edge: Red
Primaries: Green with blue tips
Underside of flight feathers: Blue-green at the bases of the inner vanes
Under wing coverts: Yellow-green
Tail: Central feathers green; lateral feathers

with yellow-green tips and red bands; the three outermost feathers also have blue bands (F, G)
Under tail coverts: Yellow-green
Beak: Light gray (P); horn-colored, tip of the upper mandible darker
Cere: Yellowish light gray
Eye ring: White (P); blue-gray (G)
Iris: Brown
Legs: Gray

Sex-related differences: *Female:* Less red on the frontal part of the head; cheeks duller; more green feathers, tips crimson (G, L)

Young: No divergent coloration known

Life in the wild: This parrot lives along the coast, above all in *Araucaria* forests. Wolters considers them as possibly conspecific with the Blue-cheeked Amazon (*Amazona dufresniana*). The Red-tailed Amazon sometimes flocks with the Red-spectacled Amazon (*Amazona pretrei*). Even though not protected, Dr. Sick reported them as extremely rare in 1969, and threatened by extinction because of deforestation (F).

Breeding: Low knows about one breeding which succeeded for Professor Riva in Brazil, albeit under nearly natural conditions. Nothing is known about breeding habits.

Remarks: Maxwell describes these amazons as good talkers and actors (L). De Grahl believes that the capacity for mimicry varies greatly among individuals.

15 brasiliensis

BLUE-CHEEKED AMAZON

16.1 *Amazona dufresniana dufresniana* (Shaw) 1812

Range: South-eastern Venezuela in the vicinity of Gran Sabana; Guyana, Surinam, and French Guiana

Red-tailed Amazon (*A. brasiliensis*).

Blue-cheeked Amazon (*A. dufresniana rhodocorytha*). While the male here shows more yellow, differences in coloration are not sex-specific.

Description:
Length: 34-36 cm.
Basic color: Dark green; underside somewhat paler; feather edges slightly blackish
Forehead: Orange-yellow
Crown, occiput: Yellow, broadly edged with dull green
Nape: Strongly blackish edging
Lores: Orange-yellow; bluish (P)
Ear coverts: Violet-blue
Sides of neck: Violet-blue
Throat: feathers have blue tips
Carpal edge: Pale yellow-green
Primaries: Black, violet-blue toward the tips of the outer vanes
Wing speculum: Precisely defined yellow-orange area across the bases of the first four secondaries
Back: Blackish edging
Tail: Green with yellow-green tips, the four outermost feathers a weak orange on the inner vane
Under tail coverts: Yellow-green
Beak: Gray with pink at the base of the upper mandible
Cere: Dark gray
Eye ring: Greenish gray (P)
Iris: Orange-red
Legs: Gray

Sex-related differences: *Female:* Wing speculum more dully colored (G)

Young: Little or no red at head and tail; forehead and lores often yellow at the edges (G)

Life in the wild: During the summer months of July and August, short flights are undertaken into the forests along the sandy coastal slopes. At other times, they keep more to the higher regions in the interior, in forests with more moderate temperatures (F). Wolters considers the Blue-cheeked Amazon possibly conspecific with the Red-tailed Amazon (*Amazona brasiliensis*).

Breeding: The only thing known about the breeding habits is that up to three eggs are laid.

16.1 *dufresniana dufresniana*

Remarks: According to McLoughlin, they exhibit quiet, pleasant behavior in captivity (L).

16.2 *Amazona dufresniana*
‡ *rhodocorytha* (Salvadori) 1891

Range: Southeast Brazil, from Alagoas and Salvador (Bahia) southward to Rio de Janeiro

Descriptions: Colors may vary on occasion
Basic color: Paler green
Forehead: Red; orange-red (P)
Crown: Red; orange-red (P)
Occiput: Dull reddish with blackish tips, partly bluish tinge
Nape: Shading to gray-green (P)
Lores: Yellowish with red
Ear coverts and rear part of cheeks: Bluish mixed with green
Cheeks: Yellowish in front
Chin: Pink-red
Throat: Pink-red
Wing speculum: Red at the bases of the first three secondaries, edges blue
Tail: Central feathers green; outer ones have a red spot on the inner vanes (L)

Beak: Dark gray, upper mandible reddish
Eye ring: Blue (P)

Young: Crown green with red; less red in the speculum—only on the first two secondaries; hardly any red on tail.

Life in the wild: This subspecies is geographically separated from the nominate form. Its numbers in eastern Brazil have declined because of deforestation, and around Rio de Janeiro it is probably no longer found. These amazons like to stay in the forest near the coast or near the mouths of rivers; in the winter they inhabit the mangrove forests. They have been observed together with Orange-winged Amazons (*Amazona amazonica*).

Breeding: Low mentions a cross with a female Lilac-crowned Amazon (*Amazona finschi*), from which two young hatched in 1972 in Tampa, Florida.

Remarks: De Grahl notes that the voice of this amazon differs radically from those of other species. From a distance, its *kaua-kaua* is said to be reminiscent of the barking of a small dog. Its manner is said to be very quiet, almost phlegmatic.

16.2 *dufresniana rhodocorytha*

SCALY-NAPED AMAZON

17.1 *Amazona mercenaria mercenaria* (Tschudi) 1844

Range: Along the eastern slope of the Andes in Peru to the mountainous regions of northern Bolivia

17.1 *mercenaria mercenaria*

Description:
Length: 34 cm.
Basic color: Green, lighter and brighter on the underside
Forehead: Light bright green
Crown, occiput, nape: Dark green, dull gray-blue edging, tips blackish
Sides of neck: Dull green with blackish edging
Cheeks: Light bright green
Carpal edge: Yellow, variably interspersed with orange-red (erroneously located by Pinter on the bend of wing)
Primaries: Green, violet-blue toward the tips
Secondaries: Green, violet-blue toward the tips
Wing speculum: Red across the bases of the first three secondaries

Scaly-naped Amazon (*A. mercenaria*).

Orange-winged Amazon (*A. amazonica*).

Back: Mealy (Bedford)
Tail: Green with yellow-green tips; lateral feathers with a red band in the middle
Tail coverts: Yellow-green
Beak: Gray with a horn-colored spot at the base of the upper mandible; broad unfeathered skin areas on both sides of the lower mandible (L)
Cere: Dark gray
Eye ring: White
Iris: Red
Legs: Greenish gray

Sex-related differences: None

Young: Presumably lacking the red speculum (L)

Life in the wild: They inhabit mountainous forest regions at altitudes from 800 to 2500 m.

Remarks: In their native area they are reputed to be good talkers (Bedford).

17.2 *Amazona mercenaria canipalliata* (Cabanis) 1885

17.2 *mercenaria canipalliata*

Range: Mountain areas of northwestern Venezuela; in Colombia in the Santa Marta Mountains and the western, central, and eastern Andes (especially near La Guayacana); in Ecuador along the eastern slope of the Andes

Description:
Wing speculum: Concealed rusty-red spots at the bases of the first three secondaries
Tail: Some red spots (P)

Life in the wild: They inhabit the forests from the tropical to the upper temperate zone. For feeding they move to the lower regions but return to sleep in the forests at higher elevations. They have even been sighted at 3500 m.; consequently, they can be considered as mountain dwellers (F).

ORANGE-WINGED AMAZON

18.1 *Amazona amazonica amazonica* (Linné) 1766

Range: Guyana; Surinam; French Guiana; Venezuela, with the exception of the mountainous region in the northwest; in Colombia predominantly east of the Andes; eastern Ecuador; eastern Peru; northern Bolivia; Brazil to the vicinity of Mato Grosso and Paraná (according to Pinter, as far as Rio de Janeiro).

Description:
Length: 30–33 cm.
Basic color: Green
Forehead: Yellow (P); blue (G); variable coloration on head
Crown: Yellow
Nape: Slightly dark edging
Lores: Violet-blue
Eye region: Violet-blue eyebrow stripe
Ear coverts: Bright green
Cheeks: Yellow in front, bright green behind

Throat: Yellow-green with blue tips
Carpal edge: Yellow-green (located erroneously by Pinter on bend of wing)
Primaries: Green, blue-violet and then black toward the tips
Secondaries: Green with blue-violet tips
Wing speculum: Orange across the bases of the first three secondaries
Back: Dark edging
Tail: Green with yellow-green tips; lateral feathers strongly spotted with orange-red, in the middle part of the feathers a dark-green band; outermost feathers blue edged (F); inner vanes red (G)
Under tail coverts: Yellow-green
Beak: Horn-colored, gray at the tip
Cere: Gray
Eye ring: Gray
Iris: Orange
Legs: Pale gray (F); gray-brown (P); horn brown (G)

Sex-related differences: *Male:* Probably more intensive blue, and at the head more yellow (G). *Female:* Probably more pronounced yellow at cheeks (G)

Young: Iris dark brown; paler coloration

Note: Specimens of the Orange-winged Amazon from northern Bolivia are usually larger, those from the Guyana countries usually smaller, than the average. Forshaw considers it incorrect to treat the smaller ones as a subspecies (*Amazona amazonica micra*).

Life in the wild: A look at the map shows the enormous range of the Orange-winged Amazon. It inhabits wooded sand hills in the plains, occurs along the rivers near the coast, is common in mangrove forests, and also is found in the woods of savannahs. Bamboo groves are the preferred roosting sites. Near Georgetown (Guyana), breeding cavities were noticed in mango trees. In northern Venezuela, it dwells exclusively along the coast, where it visits cocoa plantations. In northeastern Venezuela, its range overlaps that of the Yellow-crowned

Amazon (*Amazona ochrocephala*) which, however, prefers rather dry forests, in contrast to the Orange-winged Amazon. In Colombia, it inhabits the tropical zone east of the Andes, but in the north it also occurs west of the Andes. In Brazil, it retreats in winter into the estuarine mangroves along the coast. There, Orange-winged Amazons have frequently been observed together with Blue-cheeked Amazons (*Amazona dufresniana rhodocorytha*). According to Rehm (F), they also form small communal flocks with Blue-fronted Amazons (*Amazona aestiva*) in Mato Grosso. Elsewhere Mealy Amazons (*Amazona farinosa*) were their companions. Occasionally feeding is also done in mixed flocks. A particularly favored fruit of the Orange-winged Amazon, the hog plum (*Spondia lutea*), must be mentioned (F).

18.1 *amazonica amazonica*

Breeding: Breeding in northern Venezuela occurs in May and June, in Surinam in February and March, and in Brazil in winter (G). Nests have been found with two to five eggs; the young hatch after about twenty-one days; a nestling period of two months follows. During the observation of a nest in French Guiana, it was noted that the parents fed only twice a day, around 11 AM and 5 PM (G).

Above: Orange-winged Amazon (*A. amazonica*) in the foreground; Blue-fronted Amazon (*A. aestiva*) behind.
Left: Yellow-shouldered Amazon (*A. barbadensis*).

Yellow-shouldered Amazon (*A. barbadensis*).

The first breeding in captivity is said to have taken place in Rome in 1801, but it is not impossible that the birds were in fact Blue-fronted Amazons (*Amazona aestiva*). Between 1967 and 1974, eleven young were hatched in Tampa, Florida, in Busch Gardens. Low reports further breedings in the U.S.A.: Noegel in 1975, and Kenny in 1976. The first breeding in Germany was in 1978 for H. Mitterhuber. From three eggs, two young hatched. They opened their eyes after twenty-one days (G). In the zoo at Paignton, England, a yellow specimen of the Orange-winged Amazon was on exhibit in 1960, according to Low.

Remarks: The talking talent of this species does not appear to be anything special, but they can become quite tame.

18.2 *Amazona amazonica tobagensis* Cory

Range: The islands of Trinidad and Tobago

18.2 *amazonica tobagensis*

Description:
Wing speculum: The orange extends over the first five secondaries (only over three in the nominate form), the only distinguishing characteristic.

Note: Forshaw expresses doubts about the validity of this subspecies.

Life in the wild: On Trinidad they occur from sea level to 625 m.; on Tobago they are found in higher regions also, especially at Roxborough near Bloody Bay Street. In addition to forest areas, they frequent mangrove swamps and often choose to roost in bamboo groves. They nest principally in the trunks of dead palm trees (F).

Breeding: De Grahl speaks of a breeding season between February and June, with clutches containing up to five eggs. Nottebohm and Nottebohm (F) noted that on Trinidad egg laying usually takes place in March. A female which was observed by them incubated for twenty-one days; during this time, she left the nest only briefly, to be fed by the male on the nearest tree. During the day he remained nearby, but flew in the evening to the communal roost, probably several kilometers away. The nestling period lasted two months.

18.3 *Amazona amazonica micra* Griscom and Greenway 1941

Range: Surinam

Description:
Length: Smaller than nominate form
Beak: Narrower

Note: Forshaw does not recognize this subspecies, since the minor differences from *Amazona amazonica amazonica* do not appear to him to justify it.

18.3 *amazonica micra*

Bend of wing: Yellow
Carpal edge: Palely yellow-green
Primaries: Green, outer vanes blue toward the tips
Secondaries: Green, outer vanes blue toward the tips
Wing speculum: Red across the bases of the first four secondaries (F, G)
Under wing coverts: Blue-green
Tail: Green with yellow-green tips; lateral feathers red at bases (G) or orange-red (F); outer vanes of the outermost feathers strongly colored with blue
Under tail coverts: Yellow-green with blue
Beak: Horn-colored (F); gray-white (G)
Cere: White (L); gray
Eye ring: Gray-white (G)
Iris: Orange (F); yellow (P); yellow-brown (G); orange with yellow inner ring (L)
Legs: Pale gray

Sex-related differences: *Female:* Throat, breast, and abdomen slightly bluish; color duller

Young: Dark iris; little yellow on forehead (G); underside not yet bluish

YELLOW-SHOULDERED AMAZON

19.1 *Amazona barbadensis*
‡ *barbadensis* (Gmelin) 1788

Range: Venezuela, along the coast and on the peninsula of Paraguaná; the island of Aruba (no longer, perhaps)

Description: According to Pinter, color can vary in the direction of the Orange-winged Amazon (*Amazona amazonica*) or the Yellow-crowned Amazon (*Amazona ochrocephala*).
Length: 33 cm.
Basic color: Green; blackish edging; back and underside slightly bluish
Forehead: White
Crown: White in front, yellow toward the rear
Lores: White
Eye region: Yellow
Cheeks: Upper part yellow; lower green, strongly tinged with blue, with dark edging
Chin: Yellow (G)
Throat: Green, slightly bluish with dark edging
Thighs: Yellow

19.1 *barbadensis barbadensis*

Three specimens of the Blue-fronted Amazon *(A. aestiva aestiva),* showing possible color variation from much yellow to much blue. For this species the dark cere and bill are important distinctive marks.

Blue-fronted Amazon (*A. aestiva aestiva*).

Life in the wild: This amazon inhabits rocky, sparsely wooded mountain slopes near the coast and denser forests farther inland – dry areas, in any case (Wolters). It has not been seen on the island of Aruba since 1955; it is possible that it has become extinct there, since oil refineries have spread widely.

Breeding: Little is known about breeding behavior. Nests have been found in trees such as *Spondia lutea* and *Capparis flexuosa*, as well as in crevices and holes in rocky escarpments. No successful breedings in captivity are known; the young which hatched in 1977 for Delacour in France died after a short time (L).

19.2 *Amazona barbadensis rothschildi*
‡   (Hartert) 1893

Range: Islands off Venezuela: Bonaire, Margarita, Blanquilla

Description:
Forehead, eye region, cheeks: Less intense yellow
Bend of wing: Very little yellow, mixed with red

19.2 *barbadensis rothschildi*

Life in the wild: On the island of Bonaire they are found in the northern, hilly part, particularly in densely forested areas and in immediate proximity of the rocky escarpments. They feed predominantly on cactus fruit (e.g., organ-pipe cactus, *Cereus repandus*). They also occur in woods with cactus plants, where acacias, mangoes, *Caesalpinia*, *Bursera*, and *Achras sapota* grow, also bearing fruits they like to eat (F).

Note: Voous (F) indicated in 1957 that the differences between the nominate form and the subspecies *rothschildi* are not constant and that the characters of the Yellow-shouldered Amazons living on Aruba and Bonaire partly overlap. According to his observations, those living along the coast of Venezuela resemble sometimes one, sometimes the other type. Forshaw also concludes, based on his own observations, that no subspecies should be separated for the Yellow-shouldered Amazon.

BLUE-FRONTED AMAZON

20.1 *Amazona aestiva aestiva*
(Linné) 1758

Range: Eastern Brazil, from Piauí and Pernambuco through the southeastern Mato Grosso region to Rio Grande do Sul.

Description: Variable in size and color (G)
Length: 37 cm.
Basic color: Green, dark feather edging
Forehead: Pale blue
Crown: Yellow with white in front, sometimes blue; yellow toward the back
Nape: Blackish feather edging
Lores: Blue in front
Eye region: Yellow
Ear coverts: Yellow
Cheeks: Yellow and/or blue
Chin: Yellow

Throat: Yellow
Breast: Green, lighter toward the bottom; blue shimmer (Bedford)
Thighs: Green interspersed with yellow
Bend of wing: Red; red with yellow (L)
Primaries: Green, blue toward the tips of the outer vanes (Bedford)
Primary coverts: Dark green with violet-blue tips
Secondaries: Green, violet-blue toward the tips
Wing speculum: Red across the bases of the first five secondaries
Secondary coverts: Green with narrow yellow-green edges
Underside of flight feathers: Blue-green
Back: Blackish-edged feathers
Tail: Green with yellow-green tips; lateral feathers have a red stripe above the bases, blue-edged outer feathers
Tail coverts: Yellow-green
Beak: Dark gray
Cere: Black-gray
Eye ring: White (P); gray-blue (G)
Iris: Orange
Legs: Gray

Sex-related differences: *Female:* Not documented with certainty; according to Boosey (L), bend of wing without yellow, less intensive blue at head

20.1 *aestiva aestiva*

Young: Less blue and yellow on the head, sometimes entirely green; dark brown iris

Life in the wild: In their range, they live in the forests along rivers, as well as in cultivated areas with corn fields. Among other things, Blue-fronted Amazons also eat palm seeds; while feeding, they do not react timidly to the approach of humans. Some mixed flocking with Orange-winged Amazons (*Amazona amazonica*) has been observed.

Breeding: In the wild the breeding season occurs, depending upon the area, between October and March; in captivity, eggs have been laid as early as July. Two to five eggs are incubated for about thirty days; the nestling period lasts sixty to seventy days. The Blue-fronted Amazon has been bred in captivity often. The earliest breeding report comes from Renouard in France in 1880. In 1894, Dr. Wyss in Switzerland was successful. The Keston Farm in England had offspring in 1939, two of which bred in 1950. From E. J. Boosey of Keston Farm comes the information that in one instance the male helped to incubate. In addition, Boosey tells of a cock that could not get along with the hen with which he had been housed, and he scalped and killed her (L). In general, a Blue-fronted Amazon will accept a mate quickly.

It would be too much to list all successful breedings. The observations of Meissner from Stuttgart (G) may be of interest: The courtship of the cock followed this sequence: nodding the head, bowing, knocking the beak against a branch, giving the female a willow leaf, feeding her, nodding with spread wings, mating. An old tree trunk served as a nesting cavity. The male filled it up 30 cm. with willow twigs, leaves, and dry bits of branches. The female threw everything out again when she accepted the breeding cavity. The hen alone incubated the two eggs and was fed by the cock during this period. The young were smaller than the old birds when they left the nest and showed paler colors. They were fed by the parents for an unusually long time.

Above: Blue-fronted Amazon (*A. aestiva aestiva*).

Below: Blue-fronted Amazon (*A. aestiva xanthopteryx*).

Crossbreeding with other species has often occurred. Hybrids are known with the White-fronted Amazon (*Amazona albifrons*), the Green-cheeked Amazon (*Amazona viridigenalis*), the Double Yellow-headed Amazon (*Amazona ochrocephala oratrix*), the Yellow-naped Amazon (*Amazona ochrocephala auropalliata*), the Festive Amazon (*Amazona festiva festiva*), the Red-lored Amazon (*Amazona autumnalis*), and the Cuban Amazon (*Amazona leucocephala*). There has even been a lutino specimen. Bedford owned a female in which the usually blue feathers were white, the otherwise green ones yellow, and the red color was unchanged. Legs and beak were flesh-colored, the iris red.

Remarks: The Blue-fronted Amazon is frequently kept as a household pet in its native area. The most frequently exported of all species of amazons, it is known in many countries of the world and is kept here [in Germany] probably as much as the Grey Parrot (*Psittacus erithacus*). The assessments of talking ability and behavior with humans are variable. De Grahl reports that some not-shy animals with good imitative talent even learned songs. Low describes Blue-fronted Amazons as good talkers and entertainers; Bedford is of the same opinion, but adds that they shriek very loudly when excited and tend to bite even the best friend, either from mischievousness or jealousy. Pinter does not credit them with so much talking ability—which agrees with our experience—but describes them as pleasant and playful.

20.2 *Amazona aestiva xanthopteryx* (Berlepsch)

Range: Northern and eastern Bolivia; Brazil, in the southwestern Mato Grosso, through Paraguay, to northern Argentina near Santa Fe and somewhat to the north of Buenos Aires

Blue-fronted Amazon (*A. aestiva*), three years old.

20.2 *aestiva xanthopteryx*

Description:

Head: Blue-yellow (G); blue is more turquoise (L)

Eye area: Yellow on head sometimes only around the eyes (L)

Bend of wing: Yellow; shoulder coverts red interspersed with yellow; sometimes the red is entirely replaced by yellow.

Young: No yellow at all on head (L)

Life in the wild: In the Chaco region of southeastern Bolivia, it inhabits both moist and dry forests. According to Unger, the birds which normally live in western Paraguay migrate in the early summer to the eastern parts of the country (F).

Breeding: A cross between a male *Amazona aestiva xanthopteryx* and a female of *Amazona autumnalis salvini* occurred in 1973 for Yeats in England (L).

YELLOW-CROWNED AMAZON

21.1 *Amazona ochrocephala ochrocephala* (Gmelin)

Range: Venezuela; Guyana; Surinam; French Guiana; Trinidad; northern Brazil, in Pará at the Tapajós and in the central Amazon region; the eastern slope of the Andes in Colombia

Description:

Length: 35–37 cm.

Basic color: Green; underside paler, yellowish green

Forehead: Yellow

Crown: Narrow yellow stripe

Nape: Black edging

Lores: Sometimes has yellow

Eye area: Green between the eyes and the yellow of the crown, with single yellow feathers interspersed

Ear coverts: Bright emerald green (F)

Cheeks: Yellow-green (P); bright emerald green (F)

Thighs: Lower edge yellow (variable)

Bend of wing: Scarlet red

Carpal edge: Yellow-green

Primaries: Green, violet-blue toward the tips, inner vanes black

Secondaries: Green, violet-blue toward the tips, inner vanes black

Wing speculum: Vivid red across the outer vanes of the first four secondaries; first five secondaries with red above the bases (F)

Back: Blackish-edged feathers

21.1 *ochrocephala ochrocephala*

Tail: Central feathers green; lateral feathers with wide, yellow-green tip area, the inner vanes toward the bases a red field with yellow; outermost feathers with bluish outer vanes
Under tail coverts: Yellow-green
Beak: Black-gray with whitish orange-colored spot at the base of the upper mandible; mouth and tongue completely black
Cere: Gray with black bristles
Eye ring: Light gray
Iris: Orange with yellow inner ring
Legs: Pale blue-gray

Sex-related differences: None

Young: Little yellow on forehead and crown; less red on bend of wing; generally duller color; stronger black edging on the nape; tail has paler and less extensive color; iris dark brown, later pale yellow; beak completely gray (F)

Life in the wild: In Venezuela they inhabit tropical-zone forests. Normally they remain in the plains, but they move about and on occasion even venture into the mountainous forest regions. Yellow-crowned Amazons show much stamina in flight, covering long distances at considerable altitudes. In Surinam (where they can be found in the interior of the country as well as in the sandy coastal regions) and in northwestern Venezuela, their range overlaps that of the Orange-winged Amazon (*Amazona amazonica*), which are much more common. Yellow-crowned Amazons prefer dry forest, while the Orange-winged Amazons are found in moist forest areas. In northwestern Venezuela, the ripe fruits of the following plants, of which we know only the Latin names, are part of their diet: *Pereskia guamacho, Curatella americana*. In Guyana they live in the forest in the interior of the country, appearing only occasionally near the coast. In the northwest near Mabaruma, the Yellow-crowned Amazon is the only, but yet uncommon, amazon species. It has been observed there feeding communally with the Brown-throated Conure (*Aratinga pertinax*); the fruits of *Cochlospermum orinocense* are eaten, in addition to other items. The

species is poorly represented on the island of Trinidad. In Brazil, it is common along the Branco, a tributary of the Amazon. Along the upper stretch of the Magdalena in central Colombia, they occur on both sides of the river, preferring outstandingly tall palm trees and some kind of tree which grows over 30 m. high and bears large orange-colored blossoms. When these amazons retire to their roosts in the evening, they distribute themselves among several trees; when moving to another tree, pairs will always fly there together (F).

Breeding: In the wild, the breeding season lies between January and May. Low reports that on occasion nests have been found in termite mounds. Two to four eggs are incubated for twenty-five or twenty-nine days (L, G). The nestling period lasts for sixty-five or seventy-four days (P, G). Smith (F) describes the habits of a hand-reared, tame pair which was kept in northeastern Venezuela in semiliberty: Copulation was observed from February to April, mostly early in the morning, sometimes several times daily. Work on the nest was begun about three days after the first treading and continued sporadically for a month, usually in the morning by the female alone, while the male remained outside of the nest cavity. In three instances, three eggs were laid and only the female incubated them. The cock remained in the immediate surroundings, was frequently at the nest entrance but probably did not enter the cavity again once incubation had begun. The hen left the nest twice daily, early in the morning and in the afternoon, when she flew, together with the cock, around the nesting tree, shrieking loudly. Even before the eggs were laid, the male began to feed the female with regurgitated food, and kept this up during the entire breeding period. The eggs were infertile.

Since Yellow-crowned Amazons in captivity are generally kept as single talking birds, the small number of known breedings is understandable. A successful breeding occurred for Smith in 1970 (F). Within a week, four eggs were laid. The female began to incubate as soon as the first was laid.

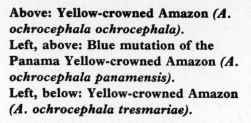

Above: Yellow-crowned Amazon *(A. ochrocephala ochrocephala).*
Left, above: Blue mutation of the Panama Yellow-crowned Amazon *(A. ochrocephala panamensis).*
Left, below: Yellow-crowned Amazon *(A. ochrocephala tresmariae).*

Panama Yellow-crowned Amazon (*A. ochrocephala panamensis*).

The following crosses with other subspecies have occurred: with the Panama Yellow-crowned Amazon (*Amazona ochrocephala panamensis*) in the U.S.A. for Latrick (Wolters), and with the Double Yellow-headed Amazon (*Amazona ochrocephala oratrix*) (G).

Remarks: All authors agree that Yellow-crowned Amazons have a good talent for talking and usually become very tame. Low noticed, as we also did, that adult birds permit only their owners to handle them and that even tame animals will bite when they become excited.

21.2 *Amazona ochrocephala xantholaema* Berlepsch

Range: The island of Marajó in the mouth of the Amazon in northern Brazil

Description:
Length: Larger than nominate form
Forehead: Clearly delineated green band

21.2 *ochrocephala xantholaema*

Crown: Yellow, continuing to the nape
Ear coverts: Yellow
Cheeks: Yellow
Thighs: Yellow
Eye ring: Yellowish (G)

Note: Only two specimens of the amazon are known; to prove the validity of the subspecies, more specimens are needed.

21.3 *Amazona ochrocephala nattereri* (Finsch)

Range: Southern Colombia; eastern Ecuador; eastern Peru; northern Bolivia; western Brazil, Acre and northwestern Mato Grosso

Description:
Length: 38 cm. (G)
Forehead, crown: Yellow band is wider than in the nominate form, but less wide than that in the Panama Yellow-crowned Amazon (*Amazona ochrocephala panamensis*)
Eye area: Yellow eyebrow stripe (G)
Ear coverts: Green with blue
Abdomen: Sometimes bluish colored

Life in the wild: It lives along the foothills of the Andes, mostly in the woods along rivers. It never moves far from the mountainous region; only along the northern border is its range somewhat more extended. Toward the south, its range reaches almost to where the southern tributaries of the Amazon begin. In central Peru they were noted along the left bank of the Apurímac in the virgin forest and a neighboring coffee plantation (F).

Note: In many books the name is occasionally given incorrectly: it is not Natter's Amazon, but Natterer's.

21.3 *ochrocephala nattereri*

21.4 *Amazona ochrocephala panamensis* (Cabanis) 1885 Panama Yellow-crowned Amazon

Range: Northern Colombia, west of the Magdalena to western Panama; on the islands Archipielago de las Perlas in the Canal Zone and on Coiba

Description:
Length: 32–33 cm.
Basic color: Feather edging not black, but blue-green
Forehead: Wide yellow
Crown: Yellow in front, blue-green behind
Lores: Yellow in front
Eye region: Blue-green above the eyes adjacent to the yellow of the forehead
Thighs: Green interspersed with some yellow (F); yellow (G)
Bend of wing: Little red (F); much red (G)
Upper tail coverts: Olive-green
Beak: Horn-colored with darker tip; mouth and tongue light or marked with black

Iris: Brown-red
Legs: Horn-colored, almost white, also partly white claws

Sex-related differences: *Male:* Eye ring is more obvious (G). *Female:* Less yellow at forehead (G)

Young: Less yellow at forehead, dark iris; beak darker, becoming light (G)

Life in the wild: In Panama, they inhabit the gallery forest and the savannahs in the lowlands. They are more frequently found on the coastal slopes toward the Pacific, only rarely on the Caribbean side, usually along rivers. In the Canal Zone, Panama Amazons cover the distance between the islands and the mainland twice daily; they fly in the mornings to their feeding places and in the afternoons back to their roosting trees. In northern Colombia, they live in the tropical zone; the Panama Amazon is the most common species of amazon there.

Breeding: First bred in the U.S.A. in 1945, Davis; first breeding success in Europe: 1963 in Denmark. In 1967, 1968, and 1969 in England,

21.4 *ochrocephala panamensis*

Yellow-naped Amazon (*A. ochrocephala auropalliata*).

Double Yellow-headed Amazon (*A. ochrocephala oratrix*).

the same pair bred successfully three times for Smith. In the meantime other breedings have been reported. In the U.S.A., for Latrick, a cross with the nominate form has taken place. The Wassenaar Zoo in Holland owns a blue mutation; in this bird, the forehead is white (L).

Remarks: The Panama Amazon is considered to be one of the tamest and most easily taught (P). In countries of their origin, the young are often raised by hand and are already tame when they are sold; because of this, their numbers have diminished during the past years. Wetmore (L) considers their voices louder than that of the Yellow-crowned Amazon (*Amazona ochrocephala ochrocephala*).

21.5 *Amazona ochrocephala auropalliata* (Lesson) Yellow-naped Amazon

Range: From southern Mexico (Oaxaca), along the Pacific slope through Guatemala, El Salvador, Honduras, and Nicaragua to northwestern Costa Rica

Description:
Length: 34 cm. (L); 39 cm. (P)
Forehead, crown: Green; blue-green (P); with individual yellow feathers (Bedford)
Nape: Yellow band (variable)
Thighs: Green (no yellow)
Bend of wing: Green (no red)
Secondary coverts: Pale yellow wing edge
Wing speculum: Red (G); with some blue (L)
Beak: Dark gray, base of upper mandible somewhat lighter
Cere: Black with black bristles
Eye ring: Gray
Iris: Orange
Legs: Light gray

Sex-related differences: *Female:* Smaller, shorter wings (G)

Young: Little or no yellow at nape; iris dark

Life in the wild: In the south of Mexico near Oaxaca they live in the tropical deciduous forest and in the humid gallery forest up to an altitude of 330 m., but are not very often found. In Guatemala and Honduras they inhabit forests and their edges in the lowlands and the Pacific coast up to an altitude of 600 m., as well as in open land, i.e., the savannah in the immediate proximity of the woods. In El Salvador, there is very little wilderness left; therefore, there is almost no suitable habitat left for amazons. In Costa Rica the Yellow-naped Amazons inhabit the arid region near the Pacific in the northwest and populate the forest which extends to the foothills of the mountain range; in addition, they are frequently found in the basin of the Tempisque, where grassland alternates with bushes and swamps. At the Gulf of Nicoya (Pacific coast), they live in the area where agriculture has been undertaken due to the greater moisture (F).

Note: The Yellow-naped Amazon has often been treated as a separate species. In northern Honduras, in the Sula Valley, there are two color variants of *Amazona ochrocephala*; some can be grouped with the Yellow-napes, while others, apparently more numerous, have a

21.5 *ochrocephala auropalliata*

21.6 *ochrocephala parvipes*

Description: Like *Amazona ochrocephala auropalliata*
Length: Smaller (L)
Bend of wing: Red (green in *auropalliata*)
Beak: Paler gray

Life in the wild: They inhabit the lowlands on the Caribbean side, not occurring above 750 m.; they also inhabit the pine savannah, moving into the neighboring rain forest for feeding.

21.7 *Amazona ochrocephala belizensis* Monroe & Howell 1966

Range: Belize (formerly British Honduras)

Description: Essentially the same as *Amazona ochrocephala oratrix*, from which only differences in color are given here
Occiput: Green with individual yellow feathers
Cheeks: Only upper part yellow
Throat: Green, sometimes a few sparse yellow feathers

Life in the wild: They live in the lowlands along the coast and in river valleys; for roosting they

yellow crown. It is possible that these represent an undescribed subspecies (F).

Breeding: Two to four eggs are usual; the incubation period lasts twenty-nine days; the nestling period, sixty-five days. In 1948, Hallstrom bred these amazons in Australia. In 1974, breeding succeeded in Sweden for Martin. In the U.S.A., a cross with a Blue-fronted Amazon (*Amazona aestiva*) occurred. Low reports a blue mutation and a lutino in the U.S.A.

Remarks: They are described as the best talkers among the amazons (P), with a quiet, lovable manner (Bedford). Their low, but not rough, voices match the human range (Low, after Slud).

21.6 *Amazona ochrocephala parvipes* Monroe & Howell 1966

Range: The islands of Roatán, Barbareta, and Guanaja; on the slope toward the Caribbean Sea in Honduras, and on the Miskitos Coast of northeastern Nicaragua

21.7 *ochrocephala belizensis*

Yellow-crowned Amazon (*A. ochrocephala tresmariae*).

prefer tall pines; in their search for food during the day, they are seen in the tall wet forests.

Breeding: In 1977 and 1978, a Double Yellow-headed Amazon—which subspecies is not quite clear—was crossed with a Yellow-crowned Amazon (*Amazona ochrocephala ochrocephala*), the nominate form; this breeding succeeded for Kenny in Tampa, Florida (L).

Remarks: In the U.S.A. they are frequently kept as pets; therefore, there are some good talkers among them. Their loud voice resembles that of the Mealy Amazon (*Amazona farinosa*).

21.8 *Amazona ochrocephala oratrix* Ridgway Double Yellow-headed Amazon

Range: Central Mexico on the Pacific slope and on the Caribbean coast in the region of Tamaulipas, east of Oaxaca, and around Tabasco; perhaps also on the Yucatan peninsula and in Belize

Description: Yellow coloration of the head is variable in its extent.
Length: 41 cm.
Forehead: Yellow
Crown: Pale yellow
Occiput: Yellow
Lores: Yellow
Eye region: Yellow
Cheeks: Pale yellow
Throat, front of neck: Yellow
Breast, abdomen: Green with blue-gray shimmer
Thighs: Yellow below
Bend of wing: Pale red interspersed with some yellow
Carpal edge: Yellow
Back: With yellow flecks (Bedford)
Beak: Yellowish white (L, G); horn-colored, gray at the base of the upper mandible (F)
Cere: Light

Above: Yellow-crowned Amazon (*A. ochrocephala belizensis*). Behind the three youngsters, which resemble *panamensis*, is an adult bird.
Right: Double Yellow-headed Amazon *(A. ochrocephala oratrix)*, 9 weeks old.

Eye ring: White
Iris: Red; orange with yellow inner ring (L)
Legs: Light brown (P)

Young: Easily confused with the Panama Yellow-crowned Amazon (*Amazona ochrocephala panamensis*); the head is green with the exception of the yellow spot of the forehead; the bend of wing is green; the carpal edge yellow-green; the beak is dark, becoming lighter; the iris, dark brown.

Note: This amazon has also been treated as a separate species. It is the northernmost representative of the amazons (G). The animals living along the Caribbean coast are usually larger than those occurring on the Pacific side; but Forshaw is of the opinion that they should not be separated into two subspecies. The larger specimens are called *Amazona ochrocephala magna* by other authors. There are only assumptions about forms intermediate with the Yellow-naped Amazon (*Amazona ochrocephala auropalliata*); in the areas where the ranges of the two subspecies meet, very few amazons occur.

Life in the wild: Small numbers live in the dense thorn forest and the tall tropical deciduous forest at the foot of the mountain ranges on the western coast of Mexico near Colima. In the east near Veracruz, they occur in arid tropical areas up to 500 m. above sea level; they seek out sources of food in the jungle, but always fly back to their roosting trees near the coast. In addition, they inhabit the forests along the rivers, as well as more open land, where woods alternate with open fields (F).

Breeding: In Belize breeding takes place in March. With breedings in captivity, eggs have been laid in May. A clutch usually will contain only two eggs. The young hatch after twenty-two to twenty-four days and remain in the nest for about another seventy days. While successful breeding first occurred in 1944 in the U.S.A., there are several reports from more recent times. Between 1966 and 1970, about twenty young were reared in the Houston Zoo (U.S.A.). For Smith in England, the same pair bred successfully three times (1970, 1971, 1972); one of these youngsters was breeding for Dalton in 1977; it had been laying eggs since 1975. Other breedings: Zürich Zoo, 1972; Williamson in Sweden, 1975; Springman in Texas, 1977. There has also been a cross with a Blue-fronted Amazon (*Amazona aestiva*).

Remarks: Among the Double Yellow-headed Amazons, many are good talkers, but there are also exceptions. Their temperament is described variously as lovable, wild, or malicious. Since these amazons are in great demand, their numbers in the wild have diminished greatly.

21.8 *ochrocephala oratrix*

21.9 *Amazona ochrocephala tresmariae* Nelson

Range: The Tres Marías island group off the coast of western Mexico

21.9 *ochrocephala tresmariae*

infertile. According to the report, the nestling had its eyes half open at the age of thirty-one days and was covered with gray down on the entire body; at forty-three days, the black iris was visible. At the age of sixty-one days, the plumage was completely green. The forehead had a yellow spot, and the bend of the wing was slightly marked with red. The red and yellow of the tail feathers appeared diluted. Its sex could not be determined. Eighty-three days after hatching, the youngster left the nest box and slept outside, a little way apart from the parents who perched together. During the breeding period, the female lost some of her usual tameness, whereas the cock had always been very shy. He took better care of the youngster than the hen once, it had left the nest box.

Description: Mostly similar to *Amazona ochrocephala oratrix*, from which only the differences are given here
Length: Longer tail
Nape: Also yellow
Breast: Upper part yellow
Abdomen: Lower part green with blue shimmer, paler green farther up
Thighs: Yellow
Bend of wing: Red with much yellow

Life in the wild: They occur on all the islands of the archipelago. It has been observed that these amazons landed in the flowering tops of the agaves, later climbed down to about 2 m. above the ground, and in the morning flew back into the forests along the coastal slopes (F).

Breeding: The only breeding report known to us comes from Zimbal, Wolfsburg, where in 1981 two animals about eight years old had offspring. Previously, at six years of age, the hen had laid three eggs. In February the first mating attempts were observed; eggs were laid at the end of March and early April; the three eggs were laid at intervals of two days. The hen incubated in a natural tree-trunk cavity; humidity was 60%. After about thirty days, one young hatched, but the other eggs were

21.10 *Amazona ochrocephala magna* Monroe & Howell 1966

Range: Mexico, on the slope toward the Atlantic coast, from Tamaulipas and San Luis Potosí through Veracruz southward to eastern Tabasco (L)

21.10 *ochrocephala magna*

A. ochrocephala panamensis, 12 years old (above);
A. ochrocephala ochrocephala, 7 years old (below).

Yellow-crowned Amazon, (*A. ochrocephala belizensis*), 7 years old.

Description:

Length: Larger than *Amazona ochrocephala oratrix*

Coloration: No blue in the plumage; otherwise like *Amazona ochrocephala oratrix*

Note: Whether this subspecies is valid remains unsettled. Low mentions it in her book *The Parrots of South America* (1972), but omits it from *Parrots, Their Care and Breeding* (1980). Forshaw does not separate it (see *Amazona ochrocephala oratrix*).

22.1 *farinosa farinosa*

MEALY AMAZON

22.1 *Amazona farinosa farinosa* (Boddaert) 1783

Range: Guyana; Surinam; French Guiana; southern Venezuela around Bolívar; the extreme southeast of Colombia; Brazil, in Amazonas, Mato Grosso, and São Paulo; northern Bolivia

Description:

Length: 38–39 cm.

Basic color: Green; upper side (back) has a mealy gray-green appearance; underside, paler green

Forehead: Yellow spot variably defined, sometimes red

Occiput, nape: Dull green, widely edged with gray-blue, tips blackish

Carpal edge: Red, frequently with yellow-green (incorrectly assigned to bend of wing by Pinter)

Primaries: Green with violet-blue tips

Secondaries: Green with violet-blue tips

Back: Powdery

Tail: Green with wide, yellow-green tips; lateral feathers sometimes slightly marked with red; extreme outer feathers edged with blue

Tail coverts: Yellow-green

Beak: Upper mandible yellow horn-colored at base, dark gray toward tip

Cere: Black-gray

Eye ring: Gray (P); white (G)

Iris: Red; orange-brown (G)

Legs: Pale gray; blackish gray (G)

Sex-related differences: None

Young: Dark brown iris; back not yet mealy; crown coloration usually absent

Life in the wild: In Colombia and southern Venezuela, they inhabit the tropical forest, but do not occur as frequently as *Amazona autumnalis salvini*, with which they are often seen. In Guyana they are at home in the lowland forest in the vicinity of the coastal rivers. Mealy Amazons will flock with other species of amazons in regions where their kind is sparsely distributed. In Guyana, for instance, where Yellow-crowned Amazons (*Amazona ochrocephala*) and, above all, Orange-winged Amazons (*Amazona amazonica*) are much more numerous, it has been observed that they even share roosts with the latter. They have also been seen together with some macaw species (F). In northern Bolivia, their range overlaps that of the subspecies *Amazona farinosa chapmani*, in Brazil that of the Blue-cheeked Amazon (*Amazona dufresniana rhodocorytha*).

Figs and the fruits of *Brosimum alicastrum* are part of the diet of the Mealy Amazon.

Breeding: No breeding in captivity is known. Usually a clutch contains three eggs. In a nest in Guyana, which was found in a tree at a height of only 3 m., it was noticed that one of the three nestlings was considerably smaller. The same was found to be true in a nest found in Guatemala.

Remarks: As a pet, the Mealy Amazon is described as a quiet, pleasant, robust, and lively bird that gets along well with others. Its talent for talking is quite considerable, the strong voice sounding less hoarse than what one is used to from other amazons; the timbre is described as noticeably soft. In the mornings and evenings, however, this species of amazon makes its natural vocalizations rather loudly (G).

22.2 *farinosa inornata*

22.2 *Amazona farinosa inornata* (Salvadori) 1891

Range: Panama and nearby small islands; Venezuela, in the northwest and in the Amazonas region in the south; Colombia, west of the Andes; to northwest Ecuador and east of the Andes to the Meta River

Description:
Basic color: Gray-green appearance of the back is less evident
Crown: Green, sometimes with single yellow feathers

Note: Separation from the nominate form is not a hundred percent valid (L, F).

Life in the wild: They live in forest regions from the tropical lowlands to the subtropical mountain regions. Of the three species of amazon which occur in Panama, the Mealy Amazon is the most common.

Breeding: In Colombia the breeding season falls in December and January.

Remarks: Bedford, writing about an animal of this subspecies in his collection, says that it was charming to other parrots, but had a loud, unmelodious voice and showed little talking ability.

22.3 *Amazona farinosa chapmani* Traylor 1958

Range: Southeastern Colombia, between the rivers Vaupés and Putumayo; the eastern slope of the Andes in Ecuador; northern Peru along the Huallaga; northeastern Bolivia

Description:
Length: Larger
Basic color: Weaker gray-green on the upper side
Crown: Green with a few yellow feathers

Note: Forshaw would prefer to synonomize this with the subspecies *Amazona farinosa*

Yellow-naped Amazon (*A. ochrocephala auropalliata*).

Mealy Amazon (*A. farinosa farinosa*).

inornata, as the coloration is the same and it is separated on the basis of its size alone.

22.4 *Amazona farinosa virenticeps* (Salvadori) 1891

Range: Nicaragua; Costa Rica; coast of western Panama

Description:
Basic color: Rather yellow-green, especially on the underside
Forehead: Tinged with blue
Crown: Green
Lores: bluish shimmer
Carpal edge: Yellow-green, sometimes slightly red
Beak: Bluish black (Bedford)

Life in the wild: In Costa Rica where their range overlaps with that of *Amazona autumnalis salvini*, they are the more common, however. They inhabit the moist wooded slopes toward the sea, being somewhat more numerous on the Caribbean side. They show a preference for the edge between forests and neighboring clearings,

22.4 *farinosa virenticeps*

as well as for plantations with large trees. They are also found in mangrove forests (G).

22.5 *Amazona farinosa guatemalae* (Sclater) 1864

Range: Southern Mexico, Belize, Guatemala, and Honduras, along the slopes toward the Caribbean Sea

Description: Resembles *Amazona farinosa virenticeps*
Forehead: Blue
Crown: Blue
Nape: Dark gray-blue (L)
Lores: Blue
Eye region: Blue onto the sides of the head
Bend of wing: Yellow-green
Beak: Black with a light spot at the base of the upper mandible
Iris: Red-brown (L)

Life in the wild: In Mexico it is the least widely distributed amazon of all the forms found there. It lives in the zone between 30 and 600 m. above sea level. Around Oaxaca

22.3 *farinosa chapmani*

22.5 *farinosa guatemalae*

they prefer the evergreen tropical forests; on the Yucatan peninsula, they inhabit the rain forest. In Honduras they are found in the mountainous rain forest up to an altitude of 1200 m., but rarely in the tropical flatlands. In Guatemala they inhabit the virgin humid forest and its edges in the Caribbean lowlands to an altitude of 350 m.

Breeding: In Guatemala breeding occurs in April and May.

Remarks: In their native area, these amazons are not considered very talented talkers; for this reason the natives do not take them from their nests. In the U.S.A., where many specimens are kept as pets, they are considered good talking birds, albeit loud ones (L).

RED-NECKED AMAZON

23. *Amazona arausiaca*
‡ **(P. L. S. Müller) 1776**

Range: The island of Dominica (Lesser Antilles)

Description:
Length: 40 cm.
Basic color: Grass-green
Forehead: Light blue to violet
Crown: Light violet-blue
Nape: Blackish edging
Lores: Violet-blue
Eye area: Light violet-blue
Cheeks: Light violet-blue in front
Throat, front of neck: Red spot, in many birds extending to upper breast
Breast: Yellow with red above (Low, after Porter)
Carpal edge: Yellow-green
Primaries: Dark green, dull violet-blue toward tips
Primary coverts: Dark green
Secondaries: Green with violet-blue tips
Wing speculum: Red with yellow on the first three secondaries; fourth, yellow with green tinge
Underside of flight feathers: Blue
Back: Blackish edging
Tail: Green with yellow-green tips; lateral feathers with red spot on inner vanes near bases (F, G); outer vanes of outermost feathers edged with blue (G)
Under tail coverts: Yellow-green
Beak: Horn-colored, tip gray; base yellowish (L)
Cere: Dark gray (P); white-gray (G)

23 *arausiaca*

Above: St. Lucia Amazon (A. versicolor). The Wildlife Preservation Trust on the Isle of Jersey is attempting to propagate rare species such as this. Left, above: Mealy Amazon (A. farinosa inornata).
Left, below: Mealy Amazon (A. farinosa guatemalae).

Red-necked Amazon (*A. arausiaca*).

Eye ring: Gray (P); pale flesh-colored (G)
Iris: Orange
Legs: Gray

Sex-related differences: *Male:* Considerably larger, probably less red on throat (de Grahl, after Porter)

Young: Brown iris

Life in the wild: It shares its range with the Imperial Amazon (*Amazona imperialis*). Both species have been frequently observed together while feeding, but the Red-necked Amazon prefers the forest on mountain slopes at lower levels and occurs even in the lowlands. According to Nichols (F), there were only about 350 specimens left in 1975; through deforestation, their habitat has shrunk. In 1979, hurricane David devastated the island, destroying their nesting sites, and wandering animals became victims of the native hunters more easily than usual. Furthermore, they compete for nesting caves with the Pearly-eyed Thrasher (*Margarops fuscatus*) (see also the Puerto-Rican Amazon). It is questionable whether this amazon has any chance of escaping extinction. The few surviving animals have retired to the north of the island around the Morne Diablotin. A lutino observed in the wild was shot and eaten.

Breeding: In the Walsrode Bird Park there are two pairs of the Red-necked Amazons, but neither from there nor any other quarter is any successful for breeding known. Thus, nothing can be reported about their breeding behavior.

Remarks: These amazons become tame when kept singly, but apparently have no imitative talent (G). Porter describes them as intelligent and playful animals (L). The temperature predominating in their native area (32 C.) is comparatively high, as is the average precipitation figure of 7.5 m. per year (G). In our climate, the otherwise lively animals appear dull and lifeless. A taste for hawthorn and elderberries has been noticed.

ST. LUCIA AMAZON

24. *Amazona versicolor*
‡ **(P. L. S. Müller) 1776**

Range: The island of St. Lucia (Lesser Antilles)

Description:
Length: 42–43 cm.
Basic color: Green, upperside strongly edged with black
Forehead: Violet-blue
Crown: Front violet-blue; pale blue toward back
Nape: Olive green, black edging
Lores: Violet-blue
Ear coverts: Pale blue
Cheeks: Upper part pale blue
Throat: Crop-band red, throat blue (G); crop blue, throat-band red to the chest (Strunden)
Breast: Brown-red, slight blackish edging, feathers are green at bases; underbelly pale green; coloration of underside varies, but is not a sexual characteristic (Jeggo)
Thighs: Pale green
Carpal edge: Yellow-green

24 *versicolor*

Primaries: Violet-blue (F); olive, violet-blue toward tips (Strunden)
Primary coverts: Green with violet-blue
Secondaries: Green, toward tips violet-blue
Wing speculum: Red (F); absent (Strunden)
Underside of flight feathers: Green-blue (F); red shimmering (Strunden)
Under wing coverts: Yellow-green with blackish edging
Back: Black edging
Tail: Dark green, underside lighter (P); green with wide yellow-green tips (F); tips yellow (G); tips white (Strunden); outermost feathers with blue stripe and red spot at bases
Tail coverts: Light yellow-green
Beak: Gray (F, P); gray-brownish, base yellowish (G, Strunden)
Cere: Black-gray
Eye ring: Light gray
Iris: Orange
Legs: Gray (light); black-brown (G)

Sex-related differences: None

Young: Less extensive and paler blue on head; iris pale brown to pale gray (F)

Note: Two reports about the St. Lucia Amazon from recent times are particularly interesting: In *Die Gefiederte Welt* (No. 100, pp. 4–6), H. Strunden gives his impression of his trip in 1975 to the island of St. Lucia and includes the reports of the chief employee of the forestry department and his staff about the St. Lucia Amazon. Strunden describes an animal held in captivity on the island, the coloration of which diverges from other descriptions. G. Mühlhaus writes extensively in *Die Voliere* (1981/2, pp. 56–58) about what he could find out on the Isle of Jersey (English Channel) from D. Jeggo, deputy curator of birds at the Wildlife Preservation Trust, about his observations of this species on St. Lucia and in zoos.

Life in the wild: In the tropical rain forest in the interior of the island, St. Lucia Amazons live in an area of barely 50 sq. km. It extends from the forested slopes of Mont Gimie toward the northwest and includes the southern part of the mountain edge Baree de l'Isle and the upper course of the river Cul de Sac. In their search for food, the amazons will appear at the forest's edge; for roosting, they retire again. According to Strunden, the following are on their menu: a kind of passion flower (local name: *pomdillion*); *paletuviér* (a sort of guttifer – this plant bears fleshy capsules with red, berry-like seeds); *gri gri*, a rose growth with fruits having pits; *bois paie marron*, a magnolia plant whose conelike fruits have seeds with a fleshy outside layer; finally, the round fruit of the daphne growth *mahot-piment* (identification by Prof. Dr. S. Vogel of the Free University, Berlin).

According to Jeggo (F), the weather strongly influences the activity of the St. Lucia Amazon; for instance, during strong rainfall, they become still and remain almost motionless, but when the sun returns, activity resumes. They are strong flyers that sometimes swoop down from great altitudes like birds of prey. Jeggo guesses that only 100 to 150 St. Lucia Amazons live on the island. Besides being hunted by the natives and deforestation in favor of agriculture and construction, they are threatened by many natural enemies. Falcons, snakes, opossums, Pearly-eyed Thrashers, and others plunder the nests (of both eggs and nestlings), and, in addition, the thrashers take over their nesting sites (see also the Puerto Rican Amazon). In 1980, hurricane Allen devastated the island severely. Only about fifty St. Lucia Amazons are left, so extinction of the species must be feared.

Breeding: The breeding season lies between January and April. Two eggs are usually found in the nest. In captivity, the St. Lucia Amazon has not yet been bred, but there is hope that the four pairs which are being kept on the island of Jersey will one day raise offspring. Regrettably, only infertile eggs have been laid so far (L).

Remarks: Bedford (L) does not consider these amazons suited to keeping in the home; he noticed that they make very loud, discordant sounds.

St. Lucia Amazon (*A. versicolor*).

St. Vincent Amazon (*A. guildingii*).

ST. VINCENT AMAZON

25. *Amazona guildingii*
‡ (Vigors) 1837

Range: The island of St. Vincent (Lesser Antilles)

Description: According to Nichols and Nichols (F), there is considerable color variation among St. Vincent Amazons. At one extreme, the plumage is predominantly yellow-brown; at the other, extensively green; and there are all possible steps in between. Here, a description of the "yellow-brown" morph is given; the differences of the green morph are noted in brackets [ ].
Length: 40–41 cm.
Basic color: Golden-, olive-, or red-brown [dark green]
Forehead: Creamy white
Crown: Creamy white in front, pale orange behind
Occiput, nape: Olive green with dull blue tinge; black tips
Lores: Creamy white
Eye region: Creamy white

25 *guildingii*

Ear coverts: Violet-blue
Cheeks: Creamy white to orange in front, violet-blue behind
Throat and sides of neck: Orange with slightly bluish tips
Abdomen: Red-brown interspersed with green, narrow blackish tips
Thighs: Red-brown [green]
Carpal edge: Orange
Primaries: Black, violet-blue in the center, yellow-orange bases [bases green]
Primary coverts: Outer feathers dark green, dull violet-blue edging; inner, green with reddish tips (P)
Secondaries: Outer violet-blue with orange-colored bases and green band in the center; inner feathers dark-green, violet-blue toward the tips
Secondary coverts: Orange-brown, green at the bases
Back coverts: Dark green, upper feathers tinged with brown, lower tinged with violet-blue and with yellowish tips
Underside of flight feathers: Yellow [green]
Under wing coverts: Smaller feathers red-brown, sometimes pale blue; edges green; larger feathers yellow [all green]
Back: Reddish brown [dark green]
Tail: Orange at the bases, violet-blue center part, wide orange-yellow tips
Upper tail coverts: Red-brown with green tips
Under tail coverts: Yellow-green
Beak: Slightly olive-green horn-colored, gray spot at base (F); whitish beak (L)
Cere: Gray
Eye region: Gray
Iris: Orange
Legs: Light gray (F); gray-brown (G)

Sex-related differences: *Female:* Somewhat smaller (G)

Young: Several authors (including Forshaw in the 1973 edition) describe the basic coloration of the plumage as green or greenish brown. In the second edition of *Parrots of the World* (1978), Forshaw points out that young green St. Vincent Amazons do not grow into yellow-brown adult animals. A green young animal, therefore, belongs to the green color morph and will keep a predominantly green coloration as an adult bird; consequently, the young of the other morph must already be yellow-brown.

Life in the wild: St. Vincent Amazons are predominantly inhabitants of the rain forest on the mountain slopes of the central massif; occasionally they occur in hilly country at lower levels, where there are nesting opportunities in large trees. They do also appear in cultivated regions but do not breed there because they are sensitive to disturbances by humans. The breeding area, which is restricted to about 30 sq. km. altogether, lies principally at altitudes between 300 and 700 m. (F). Wingate (F) reports that they are quite frequently found near settlements and show no timidity toward observers. They are reported to be comparatively loud; their direct pattern of flight was noted.

According to Kirby (F), St. Vincent Amazons like to eat the fruit of *Pouteria multiflora* and the spherical fruit of *Manikara bidentata*. Of all island species, *Amazona guildingii* is the least threatened in terms of numbers, but even its numbers have declined through hunting, deforestation, and, above all, through the continuing trade in young animals (Andrle 1973, Gochfeld 1974). The estimate of Laidler and Laidler is probably too optimistic. According to their observations in 1975–76, there are said to be several thousand specimens in the southern part of the island (L); Nichols (F), on the other hand, speaks of about 450 animals. In any case, it is to be assumed that the last volcanic eruption, in 1979, reduced their numbers further.

Breeding: Toward the end of the dry period in March and April, two eggs are laid and incubated for about twenty-five days. According to a breeding report from the zoological garden in Houston, Texas, it took sixty-seven days before the young were ready to leave the nest. In 1972, they obtained the world's first successful breeding. The female began to incubate only after the second egg was laid;

only one was fertile. Fourteen days after hatching, the nestling opened its eyes. In 1976, there were offspring for Miller in Barbados. An orange-colored female had a green chick from a predominantly green cock. In the following year two young hatched, but these died of an infectious disease after forty days (L).

Remarks: Bedford kept a seventy-year-old specimen whose fearless manner, playful behavior, and eagerness to mimic are described; however, only few *clearly* repeated words are mentioned.

MARTINIQUE AMAZON

26. *Amazona martinica*
† **Clark 1905**

Range: the island of Martinique (Lesser Antilles) (Labat)

Extinct!

26 *martinica*

Imperial Amazon (*A. imperialis*).

Vinaceous Amazon (*A. vinacea*).

IMPERIAL AMAZON

27. *Amazona imperialis*
‡ **Richmond 1899**

Range: The island of Dominica (Lesser Antilles)

Description:
Length: 45–46 cm. (largest amazon species)
Basic color: Upperside green (shiny); underside wine-red with black feather edges
Forehead: Dark red-brown with green-blue shimmer, black tips
Crown: Green-blue with red-brown bases (variable)
Occiput: Dark blue
Nape: Bluish
Lores: Red-brown to violet
Eye region: Green-blue to purple shimmer
Ear coverts: Reddish brown (F), blue-green shimmer
Cheeks: Reddish blue-gray (P); brown with blackish edging (F)
Chin, throat, breast, abdomen: Wine-red to red-brown (variable) with bluish-black edges
Thighs, flanks: Green with greenish-blue tips
Bend of wing: Green feathers with blue bases (P)
Carpal edge: Scarlet red
Primaries: Dark green (P); base green, center dull violet-blue, brown toward tips (F)
Secondaries: Green, gray-blue toward tips
Wing speculum: Scarlet red (G); dark red-brown at the bases of the first primaries (F)
Under wing coverts: Green with blue tips
Back, rump: Dark green with blackish edging
Tail: Dull dark red-brown with greenish-blue tips (F), wine-red tip-edging (G); central feathers and bases of lateral feathers covered with green
Upper tail coverts: Green with dark edging
Under tail coverts: Olive green with dull green-blue tips
Beak: Dark horn-gray, sides at base whitish
Cere: Gray
Eye ring: Gray

27 *imperialis*

Iris: Red-orange
Legs: Gray (P, F); dark horn-brown (G)

Sex-related differences: *Female:*
Considerably larger, somewhat murkier colors, according to Porter (G)

Young: Occiput and nape green; rear of cheeks flecked with green; iris, dark brown

Life in the wild: Dominica is a volcanic island 45 km. in length and 23 km. wide, with rugged mountains and steep cliffs, all densely covered with vegetation. The annual precipitation measures 7.5 m., the temperature stays near 32 C. The Imperial Amazons have retired to the forest in the mountainous central part of the island at altitudes above 625 m. (Wingate); they are found particularly on the south and southeast slopes of Morne Diablotin (Bond). Flocks have been observed also along the foothills in the northeast. In the area of Morne Anglais, some nesting cavities have been discovered (F). Natural protection is offered to this threatened species by tree ferns, vines, and palms. They live harmonously in the same area as Red-necked amazons. Imperial Amazons usually appear in pairs or in small groups, and they eat very bitter pomegranatelike fruits, seeds and fruits of palms and of the tree *Dacryodes excelsa*, as well as leaf buds. The "Sisserous," as they are called by the natives, are very shy, since they are, despite prohibition, still being shot. Their behavior after a shot has been fired is unusual: after loud warning cries have been uttered, suddenly there is absolute quiet. In general, they are very reserved about any vocalization, probably to avoid attracting attention; this is found in no other species of amazon. The hunters obtain their prey easily, especially after a natural catastrophe such as hurricane David, which devasted the island in 1979 and destroyed many food and nesting trees, leaving the confused animals roaming unprotected (Jeggo, reported by Mühlhaus in *Die Voliere* 1981/2). In 1976 Nichols (F) estimated the number of living Imperial Amazons to be 150 specimens.

Breeding: So far, breeding in captivity has not yet succeeded. The clutches consist of only one or two eggs. The natives insist that the hen pulls twigs into the nesting cavity; with the pair kept in the Walsrode Bird Park, twigs amassed in a corner of the aviary were noticed (L).

28 *violacea*

VIOLET AMAZON

28. *Amazona violacea*
†   **(Gmelin) 1788**

Range: The island of Guadeloupe (Lesser Antilles) (Du Tetre, Labat, and Brisson)

Extinct!

VINACEOUS AMAZON

29. *Amazona vinacea*
‡   **(Kuhl) 1820**

Range: Brazil, from Bahia (Salvador) in the east to Rio Grande do Sul; eastern Paraguay; northeastern Argentina, in Misiones

Description:
Length: 30–32 cm.
Basic color: Green, all feathers black edged
Forehead: Red band
Nape, sides of neck: Slightly bluish with black tips
Lores: Red
Chin: Pink
Throat: Wine-red with bluish shimmer; blackish tips
Breast: Wine-red interspersed variously with green
Abdomen: Upper feathers pale green, wine-red at the base, tips dark; lower, yellow-green with blackish tips
Carpal edge: Green, variously interspersed with red and yellow (erroneously assigned by Pinter to bend of wing)
Primaries: Green with blue tips (F); first feather with blue outer vane (G)
Wing speculum: Crimson at the bases of the first three secondaries

St. Vincent Amazon (*A. guildingii*).

29 *vinacea*

Tail: Lateral feathers green with narrow yellow-green tips; outermost red at bases with golden-yellow inner band (G)
Upper tail coverts: Pale green
Beak: Tip flesh-colored, otherwise reddish; lower mandible reddish gray
Cere: Gray
Eye ring: Light gray; brown-gray (G)
Iris: Red-brown; orange-red (G)
Legs: Pale gray (F); greenish gray (G)

Sex-related differences: (Smith, in Low, describes both sexes as identical.) *Male:* Shoulder red (L); stronger red on abdomen (P). *Female:* Larger; shoulder yellow (L); beak less red (G)

Young: Forehead and lores only weakly red (G); abdomen duller, with very little or no wine-red (P); iris dark, later murky yellow (G); beak light at first, then brown-red, then intensely red (P); iris pale, beak the same as in adult animals (Wierinckx, in Low)

Life in the wild: Vinaceous Amazons like to stay in *Araucaria* forests and prefer to eat the seeds of these trees. They have been observed repeatedly with Red-spectacled Amazons (*Amazona pretrei*) and Scaly-headed Parrots (*Pionus maximiliani*). In Argentina, they live in the subtropical forest, but also in the open plain.

Breeding: Usually two eggs are laid and incubated for twenty-eight days. Several breedings have succeeded in captivity (L): in 1971 for Smith (England); 1975 for Wierinckx (Belgium); 1978 for Gregory (Texas).

Remarks: Behavior and mimetic talent of the Vinaceous Amazons have been assessed diversely. Pinter reports that after a prolonged adaptation period they become very tame, learn to imitate sounds well, and can be counted among the best talkers. De Grahl is of the opinion that only some develop good talking capacity, but that the average bird shows no particular imitative proficiency. In manner, he considers them quiet and silent.

Vinaceous Amazon (*A. vinacea*).

Selected Bibliography

Aschenborn, Carl. 1978. *Die Papageien.* Minden: Philler Verlag.

Bedford, 12th Duke of. 1969. *Parrots and Parrot-like Birds.* Neptune; T.F.H. Publications.

Bielfeld, Horst. 1977. *Ziervögel in Haus und Voliere.* Niedernhausen, Falken-Verlag.

Davis, L. Irby. 1972. *A Field Guide to the Birds of Mexico and Central America.* Austin and London: University of Texas Press.

Deimer, Petra. *Papageien.* München o. J.: Gräfe und Unzer.

Delpy, Karl-Herbert. 1978. *Grosssittiche und Papageien.* Minden: Philler Verlag.

Enehjelm, Curt af. 1979. *Papageien.* Stuttgart: Franckh'sche Verlagshandlung.

Fischer, Rudolf. 1975. *Papageien und Sittiche.* Hannover: Schaper Verlag.

Forshaw, Joseph M., and Cooper, William T. 1973, 1978. *Parrots of the World.* Neptune: T.F.H. Publications; Melbourne: Lansdowne Press.

Gemein, Andreas. 1979. *Ein Herz für Papageien.* Hannover: Landbuch-Verlag.

Gesner, Conrad. 1669. *Vogelbuch, Originalgetreuer Nachdruck der deutschsprachigen Ausgabe von 1669.* Hannover: Schlütersche Verlagsanstalt, 1981.

Grahl, Wolfgang de. 1974. *Papageien unserer Erde II.* Hamburg: Privately printed.

———. 1976. *Papageien in Haus und Garten.* Stuttgart: Ulmer Verlag.

———. 1980–81. *Atlas Papageien und Sittiche der Welt.* Bomlitz: Horst Müller-Verlag.

Howard, Richard, and Moore, Alick. 1980. *A Complete Checklist of the Birds of the World.* Oxford: Oxford University Press.

Lorenz, Konrad. 1964. *Er redete mit dem Vieh, den Vogeln, und den Fischen.* München: dtv. [In English translation as *King Solomon's Ring.*]

Low, Rosemary. 1972. *The Parrots of South America.* London: John Gifford Ltd.

———. 1980. *Parrots, Their Care and Breeding.* Poole: Blandford Press Ltd.

Pinter, Helmut. 1979. *Handbuch der Papageienkunde.* Stuttgart: Franckh'sche Verlagshandlung.

Plath, Karl, and David, Malcolm. 1971. *This is the Parrot.* Neptune: T.F.H. Publications.

Raethel, Heinz-Sigurd. 1975. *Krankheiten der Vögel.* Stuttgart: Franckh'sche Verlagshandlung. [In English translation as *Bird Diseases.* Neptune: T.F.H. Publications.]

Ridgely, Robert S. 1976. *A Guide to the Birds of Panama.* Princeton: Princeton University Press.

Russ, Karl. 1881. *Die fremdländischen Stubenvögel, Band III: Die Papageien.* Magdeburg: Creutz'sche Verlagsbuchhandlung.

———. 1898. *Die sprechenden Papageien.* Magdeburg: Creutz'sche Verlagsbuchhandlung. [In English translation as *The Speaking Parrots.*]

Schmidt, Horst. 1978. *Sprechende und nachahmende Vögel.* Minden: Philler Verlag.

———. 1980. *Beos und andere Starenvögel.* Minden: Philler Verlag.

Periodicals:

AZ-Nachrichten. "Publication of the Central Exchange of German bird fanciers and breeders." Monthly. (G. Wittenbrock, Vor der Elm 1, 2860 Osterholz-Scharmbeck, West Germany.)

Die Gefiederte Welt. "Technical journal for bird fanciers and bird breeders." Monthly. (Verlag Eugen Ulmer, Postfach 70 05 61, 7000 Stuttgart 70, West Germany.)

Geflügel-Börse. "Publication of the Union of German thoroughbred-bird breeders." Fortnightly. (Verlag Jürgens KG, Postfach 129, 8034 Germering 1, West Germany.)

Die Voliere, "the specialist newspaper for bird breeders, keepers, and fanciers." Bimonthly. (Verlag M. & H. Schaper, Grazer Strasse 20, 3000 Hannover 81, West Germany.)

Further Reading on Amazon Parrots from T.F.H. Publications:

Bates, Henry, and Busenbark, Robert. 1959, 1978. *Parrots and Related Birds.*

Decoteau, A. E. 1980. *Handbook of Amazon Parrots.*

Greene, W. T. 1884–87, 1979. *Parrots in Captivity.*

Mulawka, Edward J. 1983. *Blue-fronted Amazon Parrots.*

———. 1981. *Taming and Training Parrots.*

———. 1982. *Yellow-fronted Amazon Parrots.*

Murphy, Kevin. 1979. *Training Your Parrot.*

Paradise, Paul. 1979. *Amazon Parrots.*

Teitler, Risa. 1979. *Taming and Training Amazon Parrots.*

Index

References in boldface indicate illustrations.

Orange-winged Amazon (*A. amazonica*), Red-lored Amazon (*A. autumnalis*).